terminal (teardrop)

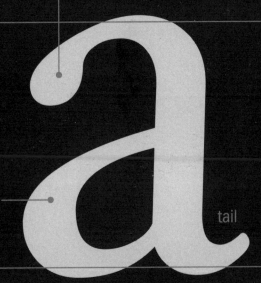

bowl

tail

type index

type index

JIM KRAUSE

HOW BOOKS

CINCINNATI, OHIO
www.howdesign.com

11   10 09 08 07   5 4 3 2

Distributed in Canada by Fraser Direct, 100 Armstrong Avenue, Georgetown, ON, Canada L7G 5S4, Tel: (905) 877-4411. Distributed in the U.K. and Europe by David & Charles, Brunel House, Newton Abbot, Devon, TQ12 4PU, England, Tel: (+44) 1626 323200, Fax: (+44) 1626 323319, E-mail: postmaster@davidandcharles.co.uk. Distributed in Australia by Capricorn Link, P.O. Box 704, Windsor, NSW 2756 Australia, Tel: (02) 4577-3555.

Library of Congress Cataloging-in-Publication Data

Krause, Jim, 1962-
  Type idea index / Jim Krause. -- 1st ed.
       p. cm.
  Includes index.
  ISBN-13: 978-1-58180-806-3 (flexibind : alk. paper)
  ISBN-10: 1-58180-806-2 (flexibind : alk. paper)
  1. Type and type-founding--Handbooks, manuals, etc. 2. Graphic design (Typography)-
-Handbooks, manuals, etc. I. Title.
  Z250.K66 2007
  686.2'24--dc22   2006023116

Cover and interior design by Jim Krause

Editor: Amy Schell
In-house Art Director: Grace Ring
Production Coordinator: Greg Nock

F+W PUBLICATIONS, INC.

Again, for my son and best friend, Evan.

About the Author
Jim Krause has worked as a designer/illustrator/
photographer in the Pacific Northwest since the 1980s.
He has produced award-winning work for clients large
and small and is the author and creator of five other
titles available from HOW Books: *Idea Index*,
Layout Index, Color Index, Design Basics Index,
Photo Idea Index and *Creative Sparks*.
WWW.JIMKRAUSEDESIGN.COM

Table of Contents

INTRODUCTION	8
1: **ENERGY**	**12**
Character studies	14
Initials and monograms	18
Word graphics	24
Logotypes and corporate signatures	28
Headlines and featured text	32
Typographic assemblages	36
Text blocks	42
Type and the page	46
Fonts used in this chapter	50
FOCUS ON: FONT SELECTION	52
2: **ELEGANCE**	**54**
Character studies	56
Initials and monograms	58
Logotypes and corporate signatures	64
Headlines and featured text	72
Typographic assemblages	78
Text blocks	82
Type and the page	86
Fonts used in this chapter	88
FOCUS ON: LETTER SPACING ADJUSTMENT	90
3: **ORDER**	**92**
Character studies	94
Initials and monograms	98
Word graphics	104
Logotypes and corporate signatures	108
Headlines and featured text	112
Typographic assemblages	114
Text blocks	120
Type and the page	124
Fonts used in this chapter	126
FOCUS ON: TARGETING AUDIENCE	128
4: **REBELLION**	**130**
Character studies	132
Initials and monograms	136
Word graphics	140
Logotypes and corporate signatures	144
Headlines and featured text	150
Typographic assemblages	156

Text blocks	160	
Type and the page	164	
Fonts used in this chapter	168	
FOCUS ON: VISUAL HIERARCHY	170	

5: **TECHNOLOGY** — 172

Character studies	174
Initials and monograms	182
Word graphics	186
Logotypes and corporate signatures	190
Headlines and featured text	196
Typographic assemblages	200
Text blocks	204
Type and the page	208
Fonts used in this chapter	210
FOCUS ON: COMBINING FONTS	212

6: **ORGANIC** — 216

Character studies	218
Initials and monograms	226
Word graphics	228
Logotypes and corporate signatures	232

Headlines and featured text	238
Typographic assemblages	242
Text blocks	246
Type and the page	252
Fonts used in this chapter	254
FOCUS ON: CORE ESSENTIALS	256

7: **SPECIFIC ERAS** — 258

Character studies	260
Initials and monograms	266
Word graphics	270
Logotypes and corporate signatures	274
Headlines and featured text	280
Typographic assemblages	284
Text blocks	290
Type and the page	294
Fonts used in this chapter	296
FOCUS ON: COLLECTING SCRAP	298

GLOSSARY	300
INDEX	306

Introduction

The inner arcade game

A designer sees something—anything from the contemporary typeface used on a CD package to a vintage VW Beetle. The image launches itself through the viewer's eyes and ricochets around inside their head like a pinball in an arcade game. As this virtual ball strikes the synaptic lights, bells and gadgets invariably found inside the head of a creative-minded person, emotional and artistic impulses, are scored. The main difference between this inner arcade game and an actual pinball table is that you don't have to put quarters into your head to start the ball rolling—it's automatic and it happens all the time.

That, in a nutshell, is the premise behind TYPE IDEA INDEX: the belief that when intriguing visuals are put before the eyes of creative individuals, fresh ideas are sparked. In the case of this book, each of the visuals being put forth has something to do with typefaces or hand-drawn letters. The 650+ type-oriented samples in the pages ahead have been custom-created to offer ideas, inspiration and information to anyone looking for ways to expand their ability to convey themes, deliver messages and communicate information through typography and design.

What this book is *not*, and what it *is*

TYPE IDEA INDEX is not a *how to* book; it's a *what if* book. TYPE IDEA INDEX—like three of its predecessors: IDEA INDEX, LAYOUT INDEX and COLOR INDEX—is chock-full of typographic samples that are designed to prompt the viewer to consider a variety of creative approaches for all kinds of design projects (in the manner of the virtual arcade game described above).

Another thing this book is *not*, is exclusively type-oriented. If you thumb through the pages of TYPE IDEA INDEX you'll see plenty of photos, illustrations, patterns and decorations that accompany and integrate themselves into the typographic samples. Why this expanded focus? It's because real world layouts very often include both typographic and non-typographic elements, and in an effort to be as designer-friendly and useable as possible, this book offers ideas pertaining not only to the use of typefaces, but to the environs in which the type is presented as well.

Suggested uses

Here are a few scattered suggestions related to using this book. Adhere to them if you like; modify them if you wish; ignore them if you'd rather. (There are no rules or commands in TYPE IDEA INDEX— only suggestions.)

Use TYPE IDEA INDEX to help brainstorm for approaches that could be applied to the typography in your design projects. Scan this book's contents for ideas that are relevant to whatever it is you are working on. Ponder each example you come across for a moment and see if anything about that sample sparks a useful notion (whether or not that notion is directly related to the sample you are looking at). Make a record of ideas that come to mind by taking notes and making thumbnail sketches as you go. Later, you can refer to these notes and sketches. They may very well ignite solution-producing chain reactions of their own.

When using TYPE IDEA INDEX as a brainstorming aid, begin your search in the chapter and section that is most closely related to the project you are working on. From there, expand your search to areas of the book that have little or nothing to do with your project. (And why not? It's well known that next to nothing is known about the strange and mysterious ways in which inspiration arises.)

Look to the samples in this book for inspiration and ideas at the beginning, in the middle or toward the end of a project.

Thumb though TYPE IDEA INDEX just for the fun of it. Not only could this be a pleasant diversion for anyone who enjoys looking at examples of typography and design, it could also add ideas to that viewer's mental stockpile of ideas—ideas that could come in handy for future projects.

You'll notice that most of the examples in this book are keyed to a small block of informational text. Refer to this text when you are interested in finding out details regarding a particular sample; ignore it when you are on a purely visual hunt for creative prompts.

And finally, always be prepared to close this book and put pen to paper or mouse to mouse pad and engage in the evolutionary creative process that brings the seeds of ideas into full bloom.

Structure

Books on typography are often structured according to outcome-oriented categories such as logo design, headline treatments, paragraph presentations, etc. Inside the chapters of books that are organized in this way, examples that convey a variety of thematic and stylistic presentations are usually featured. There are several top-notch typography books structured in this fashion, and they are worth searching for and learning from.

TYPE IDEA INDEX, however, takes a different structural approach. In fact, this book flips the previously described organizational system on its head. Here, *theme* rules and *outcomes* (logos, headlines, etc.) follow. Why this topsy-turvy system? It's simple: as just about any experienced designer can attest, concept is king. When designers create, they almost always begin by gaining a sense for the thematic feel that their creation ought to express (beginning a project without a feel for the visual personality that your creation should exude is more or less pointless; it's like getting on the freeway without knowing the name of the city to which you are driving). Once a sense for this thematic/stylistic outcome has been formed, a fitting outcome is sought.

TYPE IDEA INDEX's content, therefore, is divided into seven broad thematic categories: Energy, Elegance, Order, Rebellion, Technology, Organic and Specific Eras. Within each of these chapters you'll find sections related to a variety of typographic and design outcomes. The table of contents that precedes this introduction provides a good overview of how this structure has been applied.

At the end of each chapter is a mini-essay called a Focus Topic. These essays deal with subjects related to type, design and creativity.

If you have questions about any of the typographic terms in this book, check out the glossary that begins on page 300.

About the typefaces used in TYPE IDEA INDEX

Typefaces from over 150 different font families are featured in this book. Most of the samples appearing in its pages contain type that has been used without modifications; some samples use type that has been altered to fit the needs of a particular design (graphic elements added, characters re-proportioned, digital effects applied, etc.). Whether a sample employs letters that have been used *au-naturale*, or ones that have been customized in some way, the font(s) used for that sample are listed along the bottom of the spread in which the sample appears. At the end of each chapter a full listing of the font families used in that section are also listed.

I met my first typeface during a graphic arts class in high school and have been infatuated with them ever since. To me, a well-designed letter is the embodiment of all things artistic: form and function exquisitely blended for a specific expressive purpose. I sincerely hope that this book's contents will enhance its readers' appreciation for—and creative dexterity with—all things typographic.

Jim Krause

CHAPTER 1

Energy

Use the samples in this chapter to fuel your search for creative ways of conveying themes of **energy, motion, vitality, vigor, force** and **action** through type and its supporting compositional elements.

1,2 | Slanting shapes, overlapping forms and lively organic structures carry strong connotations of vitality. Visual artists of all kinds—including type designers—employ aesthetic components such as these to transmit expressions of energy to viewers.

3 | A letter made of strongly expansive geometric forms. *Does this typographic character remind you of any human characters that you know?* Embrace anthropomorphism when you work with type!

4 | The interior highlights of many openface* fonts radiate a sparkling sense of liveliness.

Type never just sits there. Type emits. Type is

5,6 | Expressively handwritten and typed letterforms resonate with references to their dynamic, hands-on heritage.

7,8 | Leaning letterforms (italic, oblique) are often seen as the typographic

equivalent of vocal intensity.

9,10 | Two energy-boosting visual themes that will be oft-emphasized in this chapter: the use of intense colors and large point sizes. These themes

notwithstanding, remember that the energetic conveyances of any graphic element are relative to what is going on around them.

SEE PAGES 34-35 FOR AN EXAMPLE OF A QUIETER DISPLAY OF VISUAL POTENCY.

energy. The details of every font's design carry

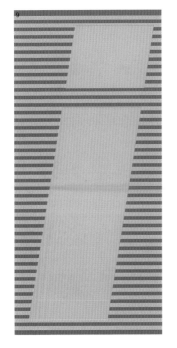

Here's a basic recipe that can be applied to even the most static letterform(s) to help them dance boldly on the page: **Enlarge, tilt** and **add color.** Consider beginning your search for zesty typographic presentations with simple treatments such as these. From there, experiment with variations, additions and radical departures. Additional energy-generating ideas can be found throughout this chapter and beyond.

1 | Before.

2 | After.

messages to the viewer in the same way that the

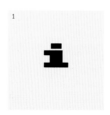

lines, curves and forms of a painting or other

Looking for ways to add visual punch to a letterform, logotype, headline, word graphic or paragraph? Consider amplifying the ambiance of your letters using concepts such as those featured here.

Keep your eyes open for other means designers use to intensify the presentation of their type. Store these ideas in your head, on paper or in your computer for future inspiration. SEE COLLECTING SCRAP, PAGE 298.

1-3 | Apply pop-art enhancements to bolster the aesthetic vigor of type. *How about employing radiating lines, pseudo shadows or a Warhol-esque stack of misaligned forms?*

work of art connects with their audience. These

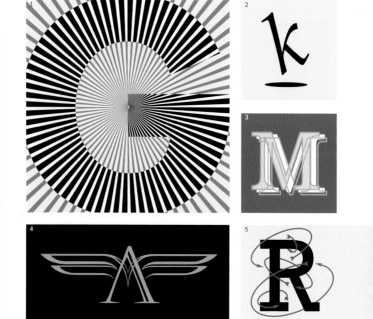

1 | Futura   2 | Palatino   3 | Century Schoolbook   4 | Castellar

4 | Consider modifying characters so that they contain—or morph into—features that exemplify action.

5 | A viewer's eye quickly falls under the spirited influence of arrows. *How about adding pointers of* *some kind to your type to lead the viewer's attention or to express movement?*

6 | Look for ways of using a repeated letterform to create a thematically relevant and visually active shape for use as an icon.

7,8 | *What about filling a letterform or word with an energetic illustration or photographic image?* Software can be used to add additional effects such as the glow around the character in example [8].

connections bypass parts of the brain that insist

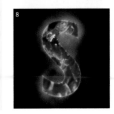

These two pages feature samples of digital treatments that can be applied to all kinds of typographic elements. Endless variations can be easily investigated using the computer. Explore!

The examples on this spread were created with the following Photoshop filters:

1 | MOTION BLUR

2 | RADIAL BLUR (SPIN)

3 | WIND BLAST

4 | RADIAL BLUR (ZOOM)

5 | LENS FLARE

6 | OCEAN RIPPLE

7 | GAUSSIAN BLUR

8 | COLOR HALFTONE

on literal meaning, striking instead synapses

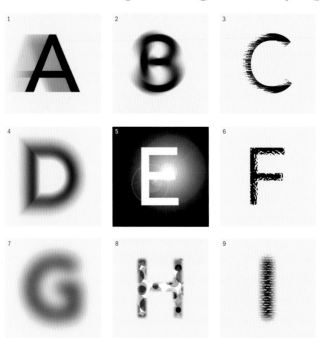

9 | BLUR + PATCHWORK

10 | DIFFERENCE CLOUDS

11 | FRAGMENT

12 | OUTER GLOW

13 | BEVEL AND EMBOSS

14 | PATTERN FILL

15 | GRADIENT FILL

16 | DIFFUSE GLOW

17 | DROP SHADOW

18 | COLOR NOISE

Note: Many typefaces are stand-alone works of art; they may not need digital assistance to improve their ability to communicate and charm. Apply digital effects sparingly and only when they are essential to a design's purpose.

that prompt emotional and intuitive reactions.

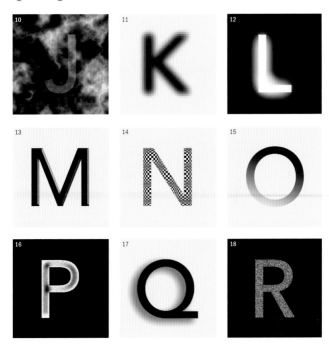

A monogram is a visual and conceptual expression that exists somewhere between a typographic logo and pictorial icon. This spread is meant to be used as idea-fuel for creating monograms that exemplify energetic themes.

1 | Without the tiny breaks in the forms of this stencil face's characters, this monogram would appear quite plain. Fonts that contain subtle notes of individuality such as this can be used to amplify the vitality of typographic designs.

2 | Use software to explore optical/digital effects such as the bulging spherical treatment that has been applied to these letters.

3 | *Is there a way of using the company's initials to create a graphic image*

Through the work of an attentive designer,

POTTER
DOANE

AERONAUTIC
RESEARCH &
DEVELOPMENT

Ward Educational
Support Services

that relates to the business' function?

4 | Mixed fonts and the use of a reversed and tilted character amount to a monogram that is both solid and spirited.

5 | Consider using non-traditional fonts and icons whose meaning is ambiguous when designing for audiences with contemporary tastes. Legibility can also be tampered with when designing for this demographic.

6-9 | When the design of your typography has been finalized, continue to explore options in how your monogram is framed, colored and embellished.

---

these abstract conveyances, combined with the

1-5 | Designers are often called upon to create type/illustration hybrids for use in layouts.

Both new and experienced designers can benefit from practicing this kind of text/image fusion as a creative exercise.

Challenge yourself to come up with visual treatments for various nouns, adjectives, verbs and adverbs. Aim for solutions that are directly related to a word's meaning, as well as for those that imply humor or irony through

treatments that contradict a word's definition.

When looking for typographic conveyances that include a visual twist, try brainstorming using lists of relevant concepts and words. Fill a page or two with thumbnail sketches

literal meaning of spirited text, can amount to

1

2

3

1 | Century Schoolbook   2 | Avenir   3 | Perpetua

based on material from these lists: quantity is as important as quality at this stage of the creative process. More often than not, the best ideas hide themselves until mediocrity has been exhausted. Use these thumbnail sketches to expand *and* narrow your search for solutions.

Why don't you make a habit of keeping a sketchbook with you? Sketchbooks are not only handy for doodles and writing—they make great platforms for exploring typographic solutions such as this kind of text/image merger. Many artists find that exercises like this are useful for relaxation as well as for building creative muscle power.

a twin-barreled blast of communicative clout.

When a visual message needs to be delivered to an audience, illustrations and photographs are usually called to center stage. As a designer, don't forget that *you* are the director of the show—why don't you give the spotlight to a certain kind of graphic element that delivers its message through both visual *and* textual means? *How about casting type in your layout's starring role?*

Experiment with solutions that use only type (as seen on this spread) as well as with ideas that incorporate illustrative or graphic additions to letterforms (as demonstrated through the previous spread's examples).

Some typefaces radiate such vitality that they

Franklin Gothic

practically shout for attention. Furthermore,

Featured here are seven straightforward approaches that could be used to infuse an all-type logo with energetic conveyances. When working on a logo, weigh the virtues of an all-type solution vs. a design that includes an icon, backdrop or framing element. *How about investigating both avenues of exploration?*

1,2 | Hand-lettered and italic typefaces are inherently energetic. Consider using a forward-leaning font for the main text and/or the subtext of your logotype.

3-5 | *How about tilting or curving the baseline of individual characters—or entire words—to add notes of excitement and individuality to a design?*

their vigor is infectious—when combined

6 | The spirited conveyances of energy in this logotype have been generated by combining characters from three distinctly different fonts. The size and position of each letter has been carefully considered—with an eye for diversity, readability and visual balance. The horizontal rule and evenly spaced row of capitals beneath the lively main text lend order to the design.

7 | *How about incorporating punctuation to add expression to a logo? Investigate both traditional and non-traditional ways of using punctuation.*

with other lively graphic elements (energetic

1-3 | Exploration is the key when it comes to creating type/image combinations that effectively honor the thematic goal of a logo. Ask yourself: *Could the logo I'm working on include an image along with its typographic elements? If so, an image of what? What styles of illustration should be considered? What sort of solution would the target audience be most likely to respond to positively?* SEE TARGETING AUDIENCE, PAGE 128.

If you are an adept illustrator, take advantage of the versatility and freedom that being able to create your own images gives you when combining type with images. Experiment broadly! If you think the image being called for lies outside your areas of artistic proficiency, you may need to look for (and possibly hire) a helping hand.

images, colors, backdrops, etc.), the result can be

1 | Clarendon, Franklin Gothic   2 | Stencil, Franklin Gothic   3 | Avenir

4 | When working with artwork that has an unrefined visual quality, how about adorning it with a font that has a similarly weathered look?

uesthetically explosive. When dynamic fonts are

4

On this spread, a selection of basic treatments has been applied to a simple headline and its subhead. Consider employing—and expanding upon—ideas such as these when seeking energetic ways of exhibiting a heading or masthead.

1 | The static sans serif font used in this sample seems to contradict the headline's message. Not the best choice for this heading.

2 | Use your pull-down type menu to explore options. *Does an italic font convey*

a more appropriate level of energy? A condensed italic font? What about using multiple weights to add visual spice?

3 | *How about using an intense hue to amplify the expression of your heading?*

featured with sedate compositional companions

1
Run for your life.
Jog your way to health and fitness in 12 weeks.

2
Run For Your **Life.**
*Jog your way to **health** and **fitness** in 12 weeks!*

3
RUN FOR YOUR LIFE!
JOG YOUR WAY TO **HEALTH** AND **FITNESS** IN 12 WEEKS.

4
RUN *for* YOUR LIFE!
Jog your way to health and fitness in 12 weeks!

An energetic font, intense color and the use of an exclamation mark can raise the volume of a headline's delivery to a virtual shout.

4,5 | Here, a pairing between a fine italic serif font and a bold sans serif face present a multitude of theme-boosting conveyances: *energy*— through the slanting forms of the italic; *solidity*—through the upright forms of the sans serif; and *diversity*—through the extreme contrasts between the two kinds of fonts used.

6 | *Why be normal?* Explore unconventional approaches as well!

7,8 | Consider modifying your headline using the filters and effects available from an image-altering program such as Photoshop.

the energy coming from the type can add a spark

5

6

7

8

There are many ways of directing a viewer's attention to important textual elements. Often, essential text is presented in a large point size, in a bright color, or within a hard-to-ignore shape or frame. Each of these methods of gathering attention is worth considering—individually or in combination with others.

Still, in the midst of all this chapter's talk about large text, bright colors and energetic visual environs, it seems worthwhile to feature a spread with this simple reminder: impact is relative. Text need not be large, colorful or framed in order to be noticed. Even a humble strip of tiny grey italic type hiding between a pair of parentheses can call attention to itself if its visual competition is kept in check.

of zest to an otherwise restrained layout

Conversely, a passive font can be infused with

(impact is relative)

Thematically, the poster designs on this spread aim for a balance between literary seriousness and kitsch amusement. These predominantly typographic layouts are intended to reflect this balance through the personalities of their fonts and the presentation of their text (size, position, orientation, composition).

In addition to taking font and compositional variables into account as you search for energetic layout ideas, experiment with the relative visual importance of each of your pieces of textual information. *What about switching the roles of your subhead and head-line? What about elevating a piece of information from worker-bee status to queen of the hive?*

notes of effervescence through its association

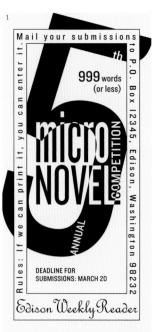

1 | Knockout, French Script (logo, each poster)   2 | Stempel Garamond

1-4 | The four layouts shown here demonstrate this sort of informational pecking-order exploration.

The first layout highlights the fact this is the fifth annual occurrence of the event. The second design features the name of the competition as its most prominent element. The third humorously plays up a restriction contained in the event's rules. The final layout gives top billing to the name of the newspaper that sponsors the competition.

Explore hierarchical options such as these—especially when working on layouts that contain several distinct blocks of text.

with lively supporting elements (forceful images,

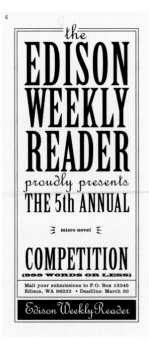

Whether designing with type alone, or with a full range of visual elements, keep in mind that some solutions succeed through aesthetic merit, some on their conceptual charms, and others through a combination of both approaches.

1-3 | Rather than *portraying* energy through their compositions, the concept-driven layouts featured here strive to *create* energy in the form of a humorous or emotional connection with the viewer. *Have you considered searching for a conceptual angle for your design?*

Concept can be king when it connects powerfully with its subjects (pun acknowledged) and rules from a throne of sound aesthetics.

playful decorations, intense coloration, etc.).

1 | actual typewritten text, Franklin Gothic   2 | Magda, Bodoni Antiqua, Franklin Gothic

When designing a layout that calls for visual

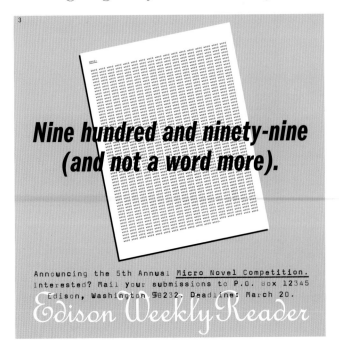

*Should **type** or **image** dominate your layout?*

This spread features a pair of designs that favor opposing answers to the question of visual domination between type and image.

1 | A colorful and jubilant photo has been given priority over the typographic elements of this layout.

Note that the woman in the image is not the only thing that's topsy-turvy in this design—the visual element that is arguably the most important (the book's title) has been featured as the cover's smallest item. Though unconventional in its presentation, the title's prominence is assured because of its conspicuous placement and unusual orientation. When applicable,

pep, use the computer to explore typeface options

1

MELINDA THOMPSON

Wrong Side ↑ Down

On August 27, 1999, computer programmer Susanne Capaletti quit her $200,000/year job, sold her Lexus, cancelled her credit cards and killed all four of her televisions. Not bad for a day's work, but she knew she could do better.

take advantage of the quirky conveyances that off-beat solutions such as this lend to their subject matter.

2 | Here, the book's title has been given more conventional visual status: *biggest and boldest*. A playful and conceptually relevant twist has been added by flipping the word **wrong** on its head. The **d** in the title's second word has been tucked into a space within the **w** above—this gives the title an extra measure of compositional strength by helping its three words appear as a singular graphic element.

Energetic inferences have been bestowed on the layout through the visually active pattern that appears behind the type and along the cover's right edge.

as well as variables in the way the design's other

2

wrong
side
down

MELINDA THOMPSON

On August 27, 1999, computer programmer Susanne Capaletti quit her $200,000/year job, sold her Lexus, cancelled her credit cards and killed all four of her televisions. Not bad for a day's work, but she knew she could do better.

Paragraphs can be infused with connotations of energy through font choice, compositional presentation, color and supporting graphic elements.

1 | A bold, poster-esque initial cap sets a colorful tone for a story being told by the legendary musician, Louis Armstrong.* The vivid contrast between the thick and thin strokes of the font's characters generates an energetic ambiance for the narrative. A lively background pattern of asterisks adds yet another level of pep to the type's presentation.

2 | A modern font—one buzzing with inferences of showbiz and nightlife—makes an intriguing connection between the old

visual and compositional elements are presented

1

Then Bojangles went into his act. His every move was a beautiful picture. I am sitting in my seat in thrilled ecstasy and delight, even in a trance. He imitated a trombone with his walking cane to his mouth, blowing out of the side of his mouth making the buzzing sound of a trombone, which I enjoyed. He told a lot of funny jokes, which everyone enjoyed immensely. Then he went into his dance and finished by skating off the stage with a silent sound and tempo. *Wow*, what an artist. I was sold on him ever since.

2

Then Bojangles went into his act. His every move was a beautiful picture. I am sitting in my seat in thrilled ecstasy and delight, even in a trance. He imitated a trombone with his walking cane to his mouth, blowing out of the side of his mouth making the buzzing sound of a trombone, which I enjoyed. He told a lot of funny jokes, which everyone enjoyed immensely. Then he went into his dance and finished by skating off the stage with a silent sound and tempo. WOW, what an artist. I was sold on him ever since.

*The text featured on pages 42-45 was borrowed from *Louis Armstrong, In His Own Words*, edited by Thomas Brothers. In this excerpt, Louis Armstrong relates his first impressions of renowned dancer and showman Bill "Bojangles" Robinson.

1 | Bodoni Poster, Bodoni Antiqua   2 | House Gothic

and the new when used in this context.

3 | The unusual use of quotation marks in this design serves as a powerful and energetic frame for the text. Many people have difficulty reading text that is lighter than its background. Sans serif fonts can also annoy readers when used for large amounts of text. If you are going to mess with rules of legibility, it's best to do it with a relatively small block of text such as this.

4 | *And speaking of messing around with axioms of proper typography, how about mixing fonts **and** point sizes? Though unconventional, this approach can draw attention to a paragraph while highlighting key words within it.*

Think of your type, images, colors, decorations

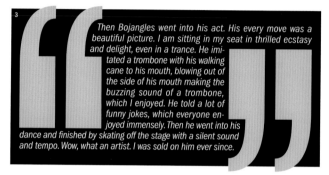

3

> Then Bojangles went into his act. His every move was a beautiful picture. I am sitting in my seat in thrilled ecstasy and delight, even in a trance. He imitated a trombone with his walking cane to his mouth, blowing out of the side of his mouth making the buzzing sound of a trombone, which I enjoyed. He told a lot of funny jokes, which everyone enjoyed immensely. Then he went into his dance and finished by skating off the stage with a silent sound and tempo. Wow, what an artist. I was sold on him ever since.

4

Then **Bojangles** went into his act. His **every move** move was a beautiful picture. I am sitting in my seat in thrilled **ecstasy** and **delight**, even in a **trance**. He imitated a trombone with his walking cane to his mouth, blowing out of the side of his mouth making the **buzzing sound** of a **trombone**, which I enjoyed. He told a lot of **funny jokes**, which everyone enjoyed **immensely**. Then he went into his dance and finished by **skating** off the stage with a silent sound and tempo. **Wow**, what an artist. I was **sold** on him **ever since**.

1 | *How about presenting your type in a way that calls to mind the animation of an expressive verbal delivery?* Though each of the fonts used here come from the same extended typeface family (Gill Sans), variety and vigor is achieved through the use of different weights, point sizes, baseline treatments and leading and kerning amounts.

    The irregular shapes of the backings behind the text add a lively graphic touch as it frames and lifts the words—ever so slightly—from the page.

and compositional decisions as independen

1

Then **Bojangles** went into his act.

His every move was a *beautiful* picture.

I am sitting in my seat in thrilled ecstasy and delight, even in a trance.

He imitated a trombone with his walking cane to his mouth, blowing out of the side of his mouth making

the buzzing sound of a trombone, which I enjoyed.

He told a lot of funny jokes, which everyone enjoyed immensely.

Then he went into his dance and finished by skating off the stage

Wow, with a silent sound and tempo.

what an artist. I was sold on him ever since.

2 | Just about every designer, at some point in their development, has spent minutes (hours?) doodling and filling the negative spaces of letters on printed material of all kinds. *Why not apply this stylistic treatment to a project, now that you're a design pro?* Experiment with a variety of fonts, fill-colors and digital effects.

evers on a rocket's control panel: Try increasing

2

Then Bojangles went into his act. His every move was a beautiful picture. I am sitting in my seat in thrilled ecstasy and delight, even in a trance. He imitated a trombone with his walking cane to his mouth, blowing out of the side of his mouth making the buzzing sound of a trombone, which I enjoyed. He told a lot of funny jokes, which everyone enjoyed immensely. Then he went into his dance and finished by skating off the stage with a silent sound and tempo. Wow, what an artist. I was sold on him ever since.

When striving for a layout that exudes energy, support the essence of your well chosen typeface with images, graphic elements, decorations, colors and compositional decisions that work cohesively toward that goal.

1-5 | Aiming for energy? Try filling a large letterform with an active image; layering type over a pattern or other type; wrapping text around a lively illustration; surrounding type elements with one or more dynamic images; or by using fonts that are designed to deliver lively conveyances. *How about skewing, scaling and tilting type and images?*

Solutions for any design problem are infinite: Use paper, pen and software to brainstorm. Experiment and explore!

and decreasing the output of each lever until the energy being delivered is enough to reach the thematic orbit you are shooting for. Keep your eyes open to how artists of all media convey vitalit

1

2

1 | Lucida Sans Typewriter, Lucida Bright, Sabon   2 | French Script, Astigma, Engravers, Sabon

"Realism can easily get in the way of reality."

ABSTRACT
ALTERNATIVES

3

through their work — these observations will

t   y   p   e   i   s
t   y   p   e   i   s
t   y   p   e   i   s
t   y   p   e   i   s
t   y   p   e   i   s
t   y   p   e   i   s

lead to solutions when you are creating energeti

t   y   p   e   i   s
t   y   p   e   i   s
t   y   p   e   i   s
t   y   p   e   i   s
t   y   p   e   i   s
t   y   p   e   i   s

Monaco

e n e r g y
e n e r g y
e n e r g y
e n e r g y
e n e r g y
e n e r g y

designs of your own.

e n e r g y
e n e r g y
e n e r g y
e n e r g y
e n e r g y
e n e r g y

Fonts used in this chapter:

One representative is shown for each typeface family.

SERIF TYPEFACES

Albertus

Berkeley Old Style

Birch

BlackOak

Bodoni Antiqua

Bodoni Poster

Caslon

Caslon Antique

Caslon Openface

CASTELLAR

Century Schoolbook

Clarendon

ENGRAVERS MT

Goudy

Lucida Bright

Mona Lisa Recut

New Century Schoolbook

Palatino

PERPETUA

Requiem

Rockwell

Sabon

Stempel Garamond

Wide Latin

SANS SERIF

Avenir

Formata

Franklin Gothic

Frutiger

Futura

Gill Sans

House Gothic

Industria

Knockout

Univers

MONOSPACE

Lucida Sans Typewriter

Monaco

SCRIPT, HANDLETTERED
AND CALLIGRAPHIC

Caflisch Script

Edwardian Script

French Script

Lucida Calligraphy

Cezanne

NOVELTY, DISPLAY

American Typewriter

APOLLO 26

Astigma

Curlz

Gypsy Switch

Magda

Postino

STENCIL

UNITED STENCIL

FOCUS ON:

Font Selection

Some designers just seem to know which typeface(s) to use for a particular layout. Others struggle with indecision each time they pull down their computer's font selection menu. So, how *do* effective designers choose fonts? The answer is a bit hard to describe—let's begin by comparing the process to medieval magic.

As a science, font selection is about as exact as the routine that witches of old reputedly followed when making pots of enchantment potion. Likely as not, the recipe and procedure that a capable designer follows when choosing a typeface goes something like this: *Bring one large cauldron of* **current trends** *to a vigorous boil. Add a pinch of* **target audience**, *a dash of* **client expectations**, *a handful of* **typographic history** *and a spoonful of* **perceived font conveyance**. *Season this mixture with a dusting of* **the designer's personal preferences** *and stir continuously until a* **chosen font** *arises from the brew.*

Sound a bit fanciful? Perhaps—though what formula for the instinctual art and science of font selection would be complete (and truthful) if it did not contain ingredients that were both quixotic and quantifiable?

Give your instinct for font selection a solid foundation by expanding and maintaining your base of typographic knowledge and awareness. Take a look at fonts from yesteryear to build an understanding of which fonts can be used to deliver conveyances of a certain era or to add a kitsch factor to a contemporary design. Looking backward at font history will reveal the identity of typefaces that have been in continuous use for decades (or centuries). It's worth knowing about fonts with such longevity in their genes, since they are also the ones that will most likely stick around for the next several decades (or centuries…).

It's also important to maintain your awareness of what is going on with typography in today's media. Magazines with contemporary content, book jackets and movie titles designed for a progressive-minded audience, and design periodicals that feature the work of the field's leaders are excellent sources of forward-thinking typographic examples. A designer who keeps her creative radar open to sources such as these gains insurance against falling out of step with typographic fashion.

A last suggestion for building a foundation for effective font selection is to keep tabs on the offerings of font companies and foundries through their online and printed catalogs. The sheer volume of fonts made available through these sources may seem overwhelming at first, but by consistently spending finite amounts of time looking through their offerings, you will begin to mentally group fonts into definite categories where they can be found when a particular need arises.

What formula for font selection would be complete (and truthful) if it did not contain ingredients that were both quixotic and quantifiable?

In summary: *When it comes to creating and boosting communicative magic through typography, use ingredients that spring from both instinctual and logical origins.*

CHAPTER 2

Elegance

Use the samples in this chapter to fuel your search for creative ways of conveying themes of **elegance, luxury, wealth, grace** and **extravagance** through type and its supporting compositional elements.

Works of art, architecture, fashion and dance convey elegance through a visual language of grace, flourish and purity of form. Typography, too, expresses itself most eloquently when it speaks through a similar vocabulary of aesthetics.

1-4 | Beautiful proportions, tastefully distributed thick and thin strokes, gracefully rendered serifs and exquisite anatomical details (such as the tails of the **Q**s featured here) characterize the letterforms of many classic roman type-

faces. These qualities make them ideal representatives of civility. Train your eye to detect the often tiny differences between the letterforms of various typefaces within this genre. Note the effect these details have on a

Curiously, themes of elegance can be conveyed

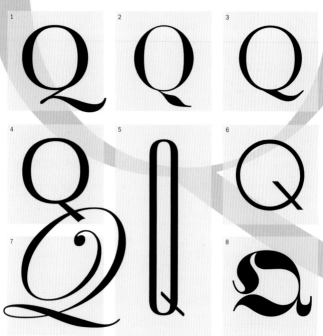

1 | Baskerville   2 | Didot   3 | Perpetua   4 | Optima   5 | Bureau Empire   6 | Futura   7 | Edwardian Script

font's projection of personality. Choose a font that echoes the persona and message of your text.

5 | *How about employing a font that possesses the extravagant qualities of a slender skyscraper—exuding excess and calling attention to itself through its striking individuality?*

6 | Consider using a thin sans serif face to channel themes of elegance through the essential simplicity of its letterforms.

7-9 | When utmost (or even over-the-top) connotations of opulence are being sought, canvass the lexicon of richly rendered blackletter, script and openface fonts for candidates.

hrough opposite visual extremes: opulent excess

9

Elegant letterforms do not need to be decorated or altered in order to deliver connotations of refinement. Still, some degree of customization is often called for when designing a cultivated logo or featured typographic element.

1-3 | A variety of ornate decorations (such as the pictorial elements used in these samples) are available as part of certain font families. Consider different ways of using images such as these to decorate letterforms.

4 | *Have you thought about adding to a letter's form to charge it with connotations of excess (and perhaps a note of whimsy, as in this case)? Experiment with swashes, swirls and graceful squiggles.*

and sparse simplicity. A lavishly decorate

1 | Requiem, Requiem Ornaments   2 | House Gothic, WebOMints   3 | Century, Hoefler Ornaments   4 | Futura

5 | Consider using software to add a thematically relevant pictorial or illustrative element to a character. Here, a photograph of a wax stamp has been superimposed over the digitally modified form of an openface character.

6 | Explore options! In this set of samples, a single typographic ornament has been used in a variety of ways to adorn and modify individual letters.

7-9 | An informally rendered serif/swash font lends a look of casual elegance to this logo. *How about creating an icon or a pattern from the first letter of a company's name? And what about applying a set of rich hues to these creations?* SEE PAGES 70-71 FOR MORE PATTERN IDEAS.

oyal bedroom and a pair of black lacquered

7

8

chopsticks could both be considered exquisit

TEN
cafe & bar

Multiple compositional and conceptual associations amplify the thematic delivery of a layout and present the viewer with layers of meaning and discovery. This layout for a menu cover serves up a number of visual and thematic connections through its typographic elements: An ornate background pattern lends notes of grace to the logo whose featured sans serif typeface might appear overly severe without the accompaniment of nearby finery; the pattern itself is made of capital **X**s—an initial that ties in with the roman numeral behind the logotype; the font used for the pattern is from the same family as the lettering below the logo's main text and a palette of richly harmonious colors has been applied throughout the design to further link its elements.

reations. The printed word, too, can express

Futura, Kuenstler Script

1 | Keep diversity in mind when creating monograms that feature letters taken from different font families. Select from typefaces that have clear differences between them and strive for a combination of characters that serve a singular thematic purpose.

2-4 | Consider different ways of connecting characters. If necessary, use software to modify letters so that they can gracefully link, lock, entwine or overlap.

5,6 | Embrace the ampersand! People who design typefaces often apply an extra measure of panache with it comes to the creation of this character. Investigate design solutions that feature the ampersand prominently

connotations of refinement through a wide spectrum

1 | Castellar, Kuenstler Script   2 | Edwardian Script, Requiem   3 | Requiem   4 | Stempel Garamond

as well as those that give this word-substitute a supporting role.

7 | *Explore the unconventional. Have you ever thought about flipping a character horizontally or vertically? Is the result legible? Does it serve a thematic purpose?*

8 | Brainstorm for ways of using a border or background shape to frame your grouped letters.

Could color or a dimensional effect enhance the presentation of your monogram?

9 | *Instead of periods or spaces, could text ornaments be used as separators between letters?*

f typographic means. The letterforms of certain

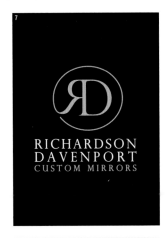

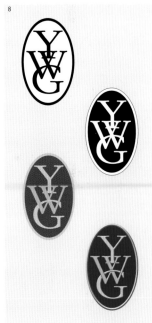

If a logo is to appropriately reflect the essence of its subject, effective typeface selection and presentation are critical.

1 | Opposites attract attention. Here, a tightly spaced, upper-and-lower-case, bold serif font is paired with its polar opposite: a widely spaced, all caps, thin sans serif face. Tactfully employed contrasts such as these can amount to a sophisticated and tasteful presentation. SEE COMBINING FONTS, PAGE 212.

2-5 | When devising a logo, evaluate the perceived personality of a variety of potential fonts. Consider different ways of separating words as well as the possibility of adding linework, an icon or background panel. Explore case: Upper, lower or

blackletter, script, calligraphic, serif and sans seri

1,2 | Bodoni Antiqua, Helvetica   3 | Albertus   4 | Copperplate   5 | Perpetua

upper and lower. Try out different baseline orientations (note the vertical **LTD** in **5**).

6 | Elegant simplicity. Letterspacing and thin weights give this sans serif font a cultivated presence.

7 | *How about removing portions of certain letters to create a uniquely minimalist presentation?*

8 | Consider digital effects. Here, the type's forms are defined only by the halo that surrounds them.

9 | B.E.E.P: Brainstorm, Explore, Experiment and Play. Investigate many avenues of letterform customization and different ways of adding graphic elements to your type.

fonts are each capable of radiating conveyances of

6

O P A L E S S E
HAIR COLOR TREATMENT

7

O P A L E S S E
HAIR COLOR TREATMENT

8

O P A L E S S E

9

OPALESSE   OPALESSE   OPALESSE

6,7 | Avenir   8 | House Gothic   9 | Bureau Empire

When a logo contains a word that has a literal meaning associated with it, consider delivering conveyances of that meaning through your design.

1 | The curved indentation in this background shape connects the name of the company with its literal meaning.

2 | Here, the company's name is framed by a solid shape while its definition is communicated through the roundness of a bold **0**.

3 | In this sample, the curved baseline of the subtext echoes the literal meaning of the main text.

Typographically, note how a modern sans serif typeface has been paired with a blackletter font from a much earlier era.

eloquence. Fonts that lack the ability to exude

1,2 | Futura   3 | Fette Fraktur, Knockout   4 | Formata, Cezanne

The result is fashionably unique.

4 | A look of faux curvature has been achieved in this design by taking advantage of this font family's wide range of available weights and condensed characters.

The addition of subtext that appears to have been written by an artistic hand adds notes of creative spontaneity to the design.

5 | *Would straightforward type best serve the look you are after?*

6,7 | *How about a more individualized approach? Sample* **[7]** *highlights the alterations made between the type in* **[5]** *and* **[6]**.

ultivated ambiance from within should not be

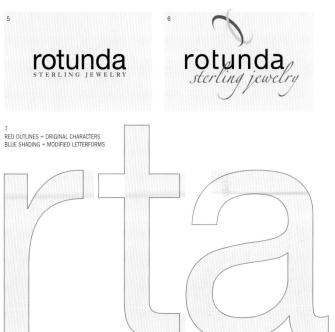

5

rotunda
STERLING JEWELRY

6

rotunda
sterling jewelry

7
RED OUTLINES = ORIGINAL CHARACTERS
BLUE SHADING = MODIFIED LETTERFORMS

rta

This spread provides a fair representation of the breadth of exploration a designer might cover *en route* to a finished logo. Use the samples here as creative fuel for your own journey toward typographic solutions.

1 | When creating a logotype, consider using unaltered or altered type (as demonstrated by the left/right pairings here). In the modified version of this pair, the **C** has been moved for a tighter fit with the **h**, and the strokes of the **h**, **d** and **s** have been altered to add verve to the type's presentation.

2 | Many openface fonts are naturally imbued with a sense of elegance. *How about filling their highlights with a rich color?*

ruled out as representatives of refinement: Theme

1

Chandeliers   *Chandeliers*

2

Chandeliers   Chandeliers

3

CHANDELIERS   CHANDELIERS

4

CHANDELIERS

1 | Zapfino   2 | Mona Lisa Recut   3 | Castellar   4 | Requiem, Requiem Ornaments

3 | Adding swashes and character extensions to a logotype can amplify conveyances of both elegance and uniqueness.

4 | Some font families contain ready-to-use decorative elements such as the ornate border seen here.

5,6 | *How about incorporating a relevant graphic element into your typographic arrangement?*

7 | In these samples, the same ornament has been used to create a decoration around one logo and a backdrop behind another. See the next spread for a set of more elaborate patterns created from this same text ornament.

of elegance can be transmitted to a font through

5

CHANDELIERS   CHANDELIERS

6

Chandeliers   Chandeliers

7

CHANDELIERS

CHANDELIERS

CHANDELIERS

One or more decorative font elements (such as the ornament featured at left) can be used to create endless decorative patterns for use as backdrops or featured design elements. Vary the orientation of the original element, its size, its relationship with its clones and the way that color is used throughout the design. Investigate solutions that are both precise and casual. *How about applying a digital effect to your pattern (a blur filter, gradation, dimensional effect, translucent layer, etc.)?*

An ornament from the WebOMints typeface.

its surroundings (a layout's ornate background

or example, can infuse a utilitarian typeface with

1-3 | There are many options to consider even when constructing simple headline arrangements such as these. Experiment widely with font choices for both the headline and subhead. Try using the upright version of a font for one, and its italic cousin for the other. Experiment with upper-case and lowercase con-figurations. Try adding linework to separate the headline and subhead. Consider alignment: centered, flush left, flush right, justified, freeform. Should the headline or subhead be letterspaced to give it a lighter feel or to help it fill its allotted space more attractively?

4 | Investigate solutions that allow the subhead's

inferences of luxury). Choosing a typeface for

1

PLATINUM SERIES WRITING INK
Won't Clog, Never Fades, Doesn't Come Cheap

2

Platinum Series Writing Ink
WON'T CLOG, NEVER FADES, DOESN'T COME CHEAP

3

Platinum Series Writing Ink
WON'T CLOG, NEVER FADES, DOESN'T COME CHEAP

4

PLATINUM SERIES WRITING INK
Won't Clog, Never Fades, Doesn't Come Cheap

1,2 | Palatino 3 | Palatino, Avenir 4,5 | Avenir, Zapfino

ascenders to encroach into the headline's territory.

5 | *How about looking for an opportune place to break the subhead so that it neatly jumps one of the header's descenders?*

6 | Here, a sans serif font has been infused with notes of eloquence by featuring it in outline form and placing it in close proximity to an elegant script.

7 | Wide letterspacing and a fine weight give this sans serif typeface a look of restrained sophistication.

8 | Consider unconventional and unexpected font pairings!

the delivery of an elegant theme is like choosing

5

Platinum Series Writing Ink
WON'T CLOG, NEVER FADES, DOESN'T COME CHEAP

6

PLATINUM SERIES **WRITING INK**
Won't clog, never fades, doesn't come cheap

7

P L A T I N U M   S E R I E S
W R I T I N G   I N K
Won't clog, never fades, doesn't come cheap

8

Platinum Series Writing Ink
Won't clog, never fades, doesn't come cheap

6 | Franklin Gothic, Edwardian Script   7 | Avenir, Kuenstler Script   8 | Fette Fraktur, Cezanne

In addition to finding ways of handling the typographic presentation of a headline/subhead, designers are often called upon to integrate these elements with images.

1 | Text legibility is the designer's first order of business when it comes to searching for a design solution that involves type and image. Search for typographic placements that integrate neatly with open areas of a photo.

2 | *How about placing the subhead above the headline for a change?*

3 | Consider a highly structured, decidedly centered layout such as this. Try out the use of a graphic element that not only

a jewel for a crown—emerald, ruby, diamond

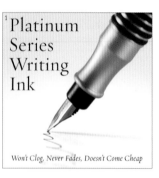

separates the headline and subhead but also adds its own note of elegance.

4 | Out-of-the-ordinary solutions are sometimes the most extra-ordinary.

5 | Though not normally found in sophisticated environs, the monospace font in this headline has been housebroken through a gracious amount of letterspacing and its association with an elegant image and a calligraphic subhead.

6 | Instead of seeing a "restriction" (such as the narrow proportions given for this poster) as a challenge, view it as an opportunity for unique typographic and layout opportunities.

pal or pearl. There are many gems to consider

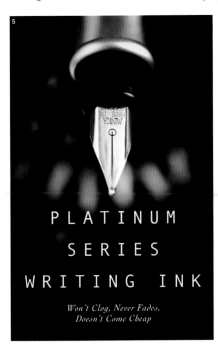

How about using a slice of highly enlarged, translucent type in the background of your design? Here, a portion of the headline adds visual activity to the image's empty space while infusing the layout with the elo- quence of its letterforms.

This poster's headline has been set in a tasteful "small caps" font. A small caps font is one that uses smaller capitals—specially designed to harmoniously coincide with the actual capitals—in the place of lowercase characters.

In printing terms, the place where an interior spread folds in half is known as "the gutter."

Be sure to allow extra space between words and characters when a gutter must be spanned

(GUTTER)

and each is capable of conveying opulence throug

PLATINUM SERIE

Won't Clog, Never Fad

by typographic elements (a feat known as "jumping the gutter"). The reduced-size layout at right shows how the type for this poster was given extra space in order to compensate for the spread's central gutter.

(GUTTER) ←

a voice that is uniquely its own. When striving

Eye-catching layouts that effectively deliver a theme and a message can be created using typographic elements—with or without the support of graphic additions. When creating a type-heavy layout such as these, carefully consider your font choices as well as their position, proportion and color.

1 | A straightforward layout created with a single font is sometimes all that's needed to attract attention and communicate information.

2 | Would a more elaborate approach do a better job at attracting notice and expressing itself? How about using multiple font families and turning certain type elements on their sides? Could a sense of depth be heightened by applying more than

for a look of elegance, set your headline, logotyp

1 | Goudy   2 | Goudy, Avenir, Kuenstler Script   3 | Bureau Empire, Bodoni Antiqua   4 | Avenir

one color or shade to the elements? What about the addition of linework that provides distinctions between different blocks of text?

3 | Try out some extreme approaches to headline

presentation. *How about using an ornate border to set the stage for your design?*

4 | *What if your layout had no clear center of interest (along with a distinct short-age of capital letters)?*

5 | Get extreme. *How about aiming for a solution that amplifies a visual theme through a dense stratum of carefully chosen type and graphic elements?*

...nd blocks of text in a variety of "suitor fonts" so that

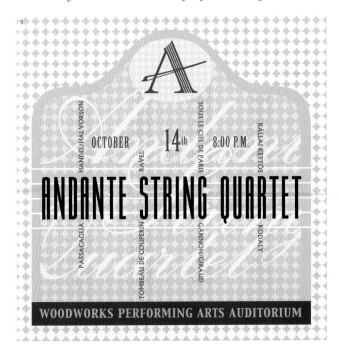

1 | Fonts that appear handcrafted make good candidates for designs that are meant to look as though they were created spontaneously. Varying the size and placement of the words and letters in this kind of layout amplifies the typeface's improvisational conveyances.

Use the computer to freely size and move words and letters until you are satisfied with the balance and presentation of your textual composition. Avoid unpleasant collisions between characters that result in areas of clutter or confusion.

you can consider the savoir faire of their presenc

1

Andante
String
Quartet
October 14 at 8pm

Sous Le Ciel De Paris ~ Gannon/Giraud

Tombeau De Couperin ~ Ravel
Passacaglia ~ Handel/Halvorson
Kállai Kettős ~ Kodály

Woodworks Performing Arts Auditorium

2 | *How about applying digital effects to further amplify the handcrafted look of a typographic composition such as this?*

To emulate the appearance of letters that have been inked upon a sheet of watercolor paper, this type was imported into Photoshop where its edges were roughened using the GLASS and WATER-PAPER filters. A blurred copy of the type was layered over-the-top to give a subtle impression of ink bleeding into the paper.

Lastly, Photoshop's TEXTUR-IZER filter was applied to the background to give it a more paper-like look.

not to mention their ability to get along gracefully

1,2 | In addition to selecting a text font that lends an appropriately refined voice to your layout, experiment with leading options. Tight leading tends to carry a down-to-business tone; wider leading can be used to imply a sense of leisure.

3 | Designers usually choose roman fonts for text blocks that are meant to speak in a cultivated manner. A sans serif font might also be considered—especially if its strokes are thin and generous leading is allowed

between lines of text. The addition of an ornament beneath this text lends an additional note of luxury to the design.

4 | If you are working with a modest amount of text, consider using a graphic

with other elements of the design) before making

1*

rk that aspires, however hum
ication in every line. And art
pt to render the highest kind c
ht the truth, manifold and one
d in its forms, in its colors, in
r and in the facts of life what
essential—their one illuminati
eir existence. The artist, then,
and makes his appeal.

2

A work that aspires, howe
justification in every line. .
attempt to render the highe
to light the truth, manifold
to find in its forms, in its c
matter and in the facts of l

3

r humbly, to the condition of
n in every line. And art itself
minded attempt to render the
visible universe, by bringing
d one, underlying its every
d in its forms, in its colors, in
aspects of matter and in the

4

to the condition of art
l art itself may be defi
highest kind of justic
e truth. ❧ Manifold a
mpt to find in its forn

The text featured on pages 82-85 is from Joseph Conrad's introduction to his memoir, **The Mirror of the Sea.**

element to indicate paragraph breaks rather than the usual indent or extra vertical space.

5 | Scripts and typographic ornaments are well worth considering when the amount of text being set is small and a look of utmost refinement is being sought.

6 | *Would spirited modifications to the text's baselines fit with your theme?*

7 | When an attractive image and an elegant font are gracefully integrated, connotations of elegance are amplified.

8 | If your layout includes multiple columns, consider separating them with decorative dividers.

your final selection. Typography is an ideal

1 | Decorative initials have long been used to establish a mood for the text that follows them. Use a character from an initials typeface or create your own. Here, an **A** from the Colonna family has been placed over a WebOMints ornament. A background shape was added to frame both of these elements.

2 | The use of small caps is another traditionally elegant way to begin a section of text. Extensive serif typeface families often include small cap fonts in one or more weights.

OPPOSITE | The black background behind this widely leaded text adds a mood of elegant formality to its rule-bending, font-shifting presentation.

receptacle—and deliverer—of elegant visual con

1

 work that aspires, however humbly, to the condition of art should carry its justification in every line. And art itself may be defined as a single-minded attempt to render the highest kind of justice to the visible universe, by bringing to light the truth, manifold and one, underlying its every aspect. It is an attempt to find in its forms, in its colors, in its light, in its shadows, in the aspects of matter and in the facts of life what of each is fundamental, what is enduring and

2

A WORK THAT ASPIRES, however humbly, to the condition of art should carry its justification in every line. And art itself may be defined as a single-minded attempt to render the highest kind of justice to the visible universe, by bringing to light the truth, manifold and one, underlying its every aspect. It is an attempt to find in its forms, in its colors, in its light, in its shadows, in the aspects of matter and in the facts of life what of each is fundamental, what is enduring and essential—their one illuminating and convincing quality—the very truth of their

1 | Colonna, Sabon   2 | Requiem   Opposite Page | Avenir, Hoefler Text

A work that aspires, however humbly, to the condition

should carry its justification in every line. And art itself m

defined as a single-minded attempt to render the highest k

yeyances. Be a letterform elitist and cultivate your

of justice to the visible universe, by bringing to light the

manifold and one, underlying its every aspect. **It is an att**

to find in its forms, in its colors, in its light, in its shad

in the aspects of matter and in the facts of life wh

each is fundamental, what is enduring and essential—

one illuminating and convincing quality—the very truth of their ex

The artist, then, like the thinker or the scientist seeks the truth and

When aiming for a design that exudes refinement, consider every visual element and compositional decision that goes into your layout. Support the essence of your elegant typeface with content, colors and aesthetics that

amount to an appropriately sophisticated result.

1,2 | Consider the relative visual importance of your typographic elements. Should they dominate the design or play supporting roles? Investigate options!

3-6 | Sometimes, elegance is brash and baroque. Other times it speaks quietly and sparingly. Explore layout ideas that address the viewer with equal parts economy and eloquence.

sense of typographic refinement. Keep your eyes open to the work of designers who have successfully captured the essence of visual grace. Look to a variety of sources—both modern and historic—for examples of exquisite

1

2

1,2 | Charlemagne, Franklin Gothic, Edwardian Script, Sabon

3

4

presented and adorned typographic designs.

5

6

Fonts used in this chapter:

One representative is shown for each typeface family.

SERIF TYPEFACES

Albertus

Baskerville

Birch

Bodoni Antiqua

CAPITALS

Caslon

Caslon Openface

CASTELLAR

Century

CHARLEMAGNE

Cochin

Colonna

COPPERPLATE

Didot

Goudy

Hoefler Text

Mona Lisa Recut

Optima

Palatino

PERPETUA

Requiem

Sabon

Stempel Garamond

SANS SERIF

Avenir

Bureau Empire

Formata

Franklin Gothic

Futura

Giotto

Helvetica

House Gothic

Knockout

MONOSPACE

Andale Mono

SCRIPT, HANDLETTERED AND CALLIGRAPHIC

Fette Fraktur

Edwardian Script

Kuenstler Script

Cezanne

Zapfino

NOVELTY, DISPLAY

Gypsy Switch

ORNAMENT FONTS
Hoefler Ornaments
Requiem Ornaments
WebOMints

Letter Spacing Adjustment

When you compose a word using your computer's keyboard, the document that contains your chosen font generates both the visible characters and the invisible spaces between the letters and words. Here, the focus is on these spaces and how they might be adjusted when a word is being used for display purposes such as a headline or logo.

After keying your headline or logo type into the computer, magnify it to nearly fill the screen. Now move back from the monitor and squint your eyes at the word (squinting helps accentuate "dark spots" and "holes" within the word—areas where characters seem too crowded or too loosely spaced). After identifying problems, return to the keyboard and begin making adjustments in letter spacing until the overall visual tone of the word appears consistent.

Rely on your eye—not a ruler—to tell you when the characters of a word are properly spaced. Try focusing on sets of three (adjacent) letters at a time; adjust the spacing within these sets until each trio appears to abide by the same standard of spacing. If you are unsure of the accuracy of your letter spacing eye, ask for feedback and assistance from experienced designers until your confidence is assured.

Adjustments in letter spacing can be made using softwares' letter spacing controls*, or by converting letterforms to paths** and moving the characters manually.

Compare the default spacing in [1] with the adjusted spacing in [2]. Squint at both samples and note the uneven visual tone of the first when compared to its modified counterpart.

Tighter than normal spacing often calls for subtle character alterations [3] that take care of awkward junctures between letters. (Characters must first be converted to paths if they are to be altered.)

Letter spacing considerations apply equally to uppercase and lowercase word formations [4, 5].

*Most programs meant for use by designers offer these controls.   **Using Illustrator, Freehand, Photoshop, etc.

KATYDID

Default letter spacing. Overall, these characters are not evenly spaced—note the discrepancy between the spacing of the characters within [a] and [b].

KATYDID

Adjusted spacing. Now the visual tone of the word appears consistent. Allow characters to touch [c] if it helps achieve even visual spacing throughout the word. Adjustments such as these can be subtle: the light blue characters in the sample below indicate the position of the original letterforms before they were moved.

KATYDID

KATYDID

Tight spacing. The serifs of the **T** and **Y** have been sculpted to make an artful junction of their meeting [d]. When necessary, make adjustments such as these while maintaining each character's legibility.

Katydid

Note how the default spacing has made distinct visual groups out of the letters in [g] and [h]. Try squinting at this sample to make these groups stand out more clearly.

Katydid

After adjusting the letter spacing, the serif on the **K**s diagonal stem was shortened [i] so that it would not awkwardly crowd the **a** (which has been moved slightly to the left).

CHAPTER 3

Order

Projecting themes of **order, balance, regularity** and **stability** through type and its supporting compositional elements.

The disciplined forms of the seven sans serif characters featured on this spread make them ideal representatives of the themes of this chapter: order, balance, regularity and stability. Designers often choose lean and functional sans serif faces such as these when aiming for conveyances of utmost clarity and punctuality.

1-3 | To the casual observer, many sans serif fonts appear virtually identical. A good place to look for notes of individuality among these related faces is in the termination of their strokes. Note the different angles at which the terminals of these three letterforms have been cut. Cultivate the ability to discern the variances in persona that tiny details

When designing for clients who deal in pragmati

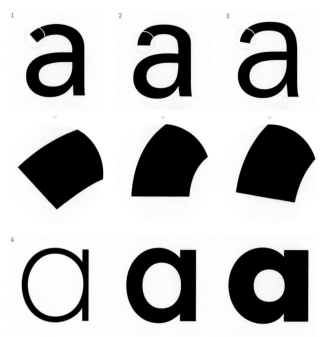

1 | Avenir   2 | Univers   3 | Franklin Gothic   4 | Futura   Opposite page | Helvetica

such as these can project—especially when they are multiplied by the thousands of characters on a typical page of text.

4 | Other sans serif fonts have a whole different way of saying "**a**."

THIS PAGE | Because of their apparent simplicity, many viewers overlook the exquisite aesthetics of sans serif letterforms. Take a moment to enjoy the subtly sculpted forms of this Helvetica **a** (designed by Edouard Hoffmann and Max Miedinger in 1957). *Are you surprised by the graceful expansion and tapering of its strokes as they transition from one part of the letter to another?* And what about those negative spaces! Beautiful, inspirational, instructive.

ervices and products, the first order of business is

The exclusive featuring of sans serif fonts on the previous spread is not meant to imply that letters of that genre are the only ones able to speak with voices of order and authority. Serif typefaces, too, especially those that exude conveyances of their historical lineage (such as the font featured below—a twentieth century version of a face designed by Claude Garamond in the late 1500s) are also capable of projecting a trustworthy ambiance. In fact, certain typefaces, presented in an orderly and concise manner, seem able to lend credence to even the most absurd claims (a fact that has not been overlooked by advertisers since the earliest days of print).

usually order itself. Firms involved in finance

The world is

Stempel Garamond

medicine, science and law often ask their target

flat.

Connotations of order can be amplified through associations between tidy graphic elements and type. Consider using the concepts that have been applied to the single-letter designs on this spread when seeking conveyances of precision and regularity for any kind of typographic composition.

1 | Neat linework and simple shapes can be used to establish orderly environs for type. *How about using line and type weights that contrast with each other?*

What about using letter/line weights that appear the same?

2 | Bold, simple shapes can be used to frame and bring a sense of discipline to a rambunctious font.

audience (through visual media) to conside

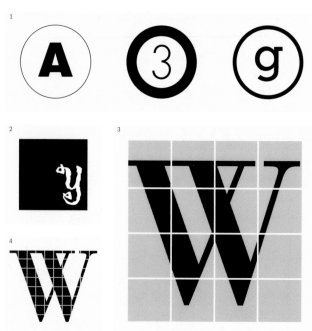

1 | Futura, Helvetica, Rockwell   2 | Hollyweird   3,4 | Bodoni Antiqua

3,4 | Consider using a grid behind—or within—typographic elements to project connotations of structure and organization.

5 | Consistency and balance connote order. The neatly centered type in this logo comes from a single font family—including the tilted **c** being used as an icon above the logotype.

6-9 | Type can by visually engaged with technical (or pseudo-technical) graphic elements to infuse designs with notes of planning and precision.

10 | Punctuation can add a sense of containment and finality to a textual element by virtue of its compositional presence *and* textual significance.

erious matters such as investments, medical

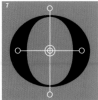

1 | Balance, harmony, regularity and organization: Architects, interior decorators and sculptors call on attributes such as these when seeking connotations of order for their creations. Not surprisingly, these same qualities can be employed by graphic designers when seeking a sense of stability for their typographic structures.

2 | As the saying goes, good fences make good neighbors. Here, a potential clash of font personalities is averted by placing the hi-tech characters of a monogram inside a colored rectangular shape that neatly separates it from the utilitarian font used for the company name. Consider using tactics such as this to keep

treatments and legal assistance. Therefore, th

1 | Franklin Gothic   2 | Buzzer Three, News Gothic   3 | Univers

visual dissension from arising between contrasting fonts of your orderly typographic composition.

3-5 | Keep your eyes and mind open to opportunistic letterform mergers and associations—certain letter combinations offer unique design opportunities. If necessary, convert characters to paths so that they can be altered to achieve a letter-perfect fit.

6-8 | One font, five potential monogram solutions.

A sense of order is established in each of these designs through compositions that favor the criteria described at the beginning of this spread: balance, harmony, regularity and organization.

ids, brochures, packaging, posters and web pages

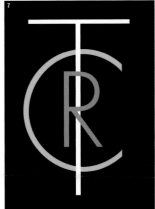

Orderly and offbeat compositional themes can work together harmoniously to achieve thematic middle ground between formal aspects of the business world and informal characteristics of a particular business.

1 | In this design, a carefully crafted monogram and compositional symmetry lend a sense of discipline to the offbeat influences of a radically condensed typeface, angled baselines and a lively background pattern.

2,3 | A harmonious connection between the monogram and its backdrop were sought for the center portion of the logo featured below. To achieve this visual accord, a detail from within the monogram **[2]** was used as the basis for the

that deliver these messages need to be presente

1

background pattern [3].
It is far from mandatory
to come up with pattern-
building components in
this way, but it is an
approach worth consider-
ing if harmony-enhancing
expressions are being
sought for a design.

n a way that gains the viewer's confidence

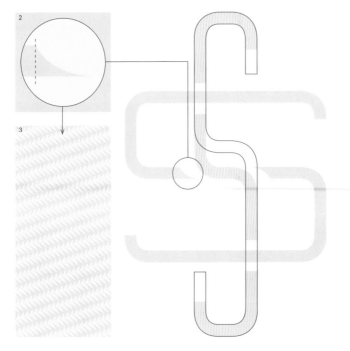

Consider these four ways of applying ORDER to a word graphic:

1 | ORDER as *general topic*. Here, theme-boosting images and a custom typographic twist are applied to a word with orderly connotations. When aiming for this kind of typographic expression, seek a font whose letterforms will support the design's goals in terms of its concept and compositional structure.

2 | ORDER as *theme enforcer*. Symmetry is an aesthetic means of conveying order and balance. In this sample, the word "symmetry" serves as its own subject-matter for a demonstrative graphic.

and trust. As one might expect, connotations ₐ

1 | Knockout   2 | Edwardian Script

How about exploring themes such as pattern, rotation, balance and harmony through word graphics of your own?

3 | ORDER as *theme generator*. Callouts are ripe with inferences of organization.

Sometimes callouts are applied for informational purposes; sometimes their role is thematic or decorative. In addition to callouts, consider other visuals that could be used to generate orderly themes: grids, precise patterns, linework, etc.

4 | ORDER as a *design approach*. Could a hypermethodical arrangement of your composition's elements be employed to enhance the delivery of its message and to attract viewers' notice?

rustworthiness and stability can be delivered

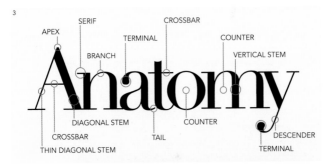

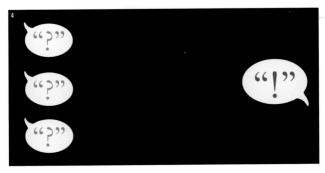

Here, photography and type have been joined with an orderly concept (file folders = organization incarnate). Designers often create thematically inclined images such as this for use on book jackets, presentation folders, web pages, posters, brochures and advertisements. *How about applying an image + typography approach to a project of yours?* (Production note: The type in this image was superimposed over blank file folders using LAYER controls in Photoshop.)

through designs that are cleanly organized and

Everything

Century Schoolbook

characterized by balance, regularity and harmony.

in its place.

LOGOTYPES AND CORPORATE SIGNATURES

ORDER

Straightforward logotype solutions are often perfectly suited for straight-laced businesses such as the one being designed for on this spread.

1 | Begin with a thorough survey of font options.

Which typefaces best reflect the personality and purpose of your client's business?

2-4 | Once your search for an appropriate font has been narrowed to a few favorites, begin exploring

alignment, style and case options. Evaluate the merits of each against the visual and thematic goals of the design.

5 | You can force words of different widths into a justified arrangement by varying

The typefaces that designers choose to inhabit thi

Granville Employment Agency	Granville Employment Agency	Granville Employment Agency

Granville Employment Agency (italic, three variations)

GRANVILLE EMPLOYMENT AGENCY (caps, three variations)

108

1 | mixed fonts   2-6 | Hoefler

either the kerning or the size of each word. In the case of these particular words, neither technique works very well. The first method results in excessive space between letters of the word **agency**; the second approach grants too

much visual status to a word that doesn't deserve it. The next sample offers a potential solution.

6 | Consider using linework to give your ragged word-group a pseudo-justified appearance.

7-9 | *Instead of stacking the type, how about setting it horizontally?* Experiment with font choices, variations in word and letter spacing, the use of different weights of type, and the incorporation of linework and panels.

class of layout are usually straightforward, highly

5

GRANVILLE
EMPLOYMENT
A G E N C Y

⊘

GRANVILLE
EMPLOYMENT
AGENCY

6

GRANVILLE
EMPLOYMENT
AGENCY

7

Granville Employment Agency

8

Granville**Employment**Agency

9

GRANVILLE EMPLOYMENT AGENCY

Expanding upon the last spread's exploration of logos designed within the framework of orderly themes, graphic elements have been added to this series of examples.

1,2 | Repetition can be employed to deliver connotations of consistency. Linework is used to lend these themes to the type in the first sample; a series of rectangular panels is used for the same purposes in the second design.

3,4 | Icons have been joined with the type in these logos to enhance the meaning and vitality of their presentation. The balanced and neat rendering of these additions helps ensure that the logo's overarching

legible, and free of the quirks exemplified b

1

2

3

4

5

6

1,2 | Lucida Sans Typewriter   3,4 | Avenir   5,6 | Bodoni Antiqua

conveyances of order are upheld.

5 | Exact framing connotes organization. In this sample, the tiny corner marks around the type give the logo a look of accuracy and sparse precision.

6 | Here again, the logotype has been contained within a graphic element. In this case, the border is reminiscent of the label on a file cabinet's drawers—a theme that connects well with the company's persona.

Brainstorm for ideas when searching for a thematically relevant graphic addition for a logo.

7 | Logos are layouts—use the computer to widely explore compositional options!

onts suited for zanier themes. Still, a typeface

7

Use these billboard layouts to help brainstorm for headline treatments for any kind of project that calls for an orderly delivery of its primary message.

Since the product being promoted here is a natural medicine, a mix of two the-matic projections has been sought for each design: congenial warmth and authoritative credibility.

1 | Here, the casual presentation of an amicable serif font is counterbalanced by the orderliness conveyed through its conscientious grouping and centered alignment.

2 | In this design, a no-nonsense headline presentation has been teasingly interrupted by an image of the product.

does not need to be sterile in order to thrive i

3,4 | A look of validity can be enforced through visible structural elements such as the panels that neatly separate and organize the type in these designs. The exaggerated presentation of the bold sans serif headlines is meant to appear somewhat over-the-top—not exactly humorous, though not quite serious, either.

5,6 | Historically, medicinal packaging has often blended complementary themes of authority and warmth. The precise structure of these layouts enforces a sense of proficiency, while the addition of nature-oriented text ornaments lends notes of healing and humanity. *Could complementary themes such as these be used to deepen the message of a project of yours?*

he fastidious world of straight-laced design.

On this spread and the next, business card layouts (actual size) are used as the basis for explorations of orderly typographic assemblages. When the amount of information required on a card is as substantial as this, compositional decisions need to be made that will help avoid clutter and confusion.

1 | Order and simplicity often go hand in hand; what could be more simple than a centered typographic solution such as this? Use font weights, sizes, colors and spacing to divide the typographic layouts such as this into distinct groups of related information.

A subtle accent of creativity is lent to this design by the ghosted monogram in the background.

There are many typefaces that are both neatl

1

AKIZAWA DATA RECOVERY
On-site Data Recovery since 1999

John H. Smith
Vice President

1234 56th Avenue Northwest, Suite 4061
Seattle, Washington 98225
Wk: 206.765.4321 | Cel: 206.123.4567
john@akizawadata.com

AKIZAWADATA.COM

2

AKIZAWA ADR
DATA RECOVERY

John H. Smith	1234 56th Ave. N.W., #4061
Vice President	Seattle, Washington 98225
	Wk: 206.765.4321
john@akizawadata.com	Cel: 206.123.4567
AKIZAWADATA.COM	ON-SITE DATA RECOVERY SINCE 1999

2 | *Linework, anyone? Color? Panels? Tints? Overprinting and reversed type? All of the above? Simplicity is not the only route to typographic order.*

3,4 | These samples project a clear sense of order through cleanly aligned and distributed typographic elements.

Subtle differences between these two layouts illustrate a number of avenues worthy of exploration. Take a close look at the ways that baselines, color breaks, columns and linework align within each composition. Note how certain words are sometimes abbreviated, expanded or moved to a different position to serve the compositional interests of the layout.

endered and reverberating with thematic

3

**AKIZAWA
DATA RECOVERY**
*On-site Data Recovery
since 1999*

John H. Smith
Vice President

1234 56th Avenue Northwest
Suite 4061
Seattle, Washington 98225

Wk: 206.765.4321
Cel: 206.123.4567

john@akizawadata.com

4

AKIZAWA DATA RECOVERY

John H. Smith *Vice President*

1234 56th Ave. N.W., #4061
Seattle, Washington 98225
Wk: 206.765.4321
Cel: 206.123.4567

john@akizawadata.com

AKIZAWADATA.COM
On-site Data Recovery since 1999

Printed letterforms, and the invisible conveyances of the text they populate, reach the mind of the viewer through the visual, physical, dimensional and tactile world of paper and ink. These tangible characteristics have a significant impact on the thematic and aesthetic assets of a design's typography.

As a designer, don't forget to consider variables such as these as you compose your layout. Talk with your printer about additional production possibilities such as embossing, foil-stamping, die cutting and drilling. Keep your eyes open to ways other designers are using paper, ink and bindery options to enhance the presentation of their pieces.

nuances of warmth, creativity or modernity

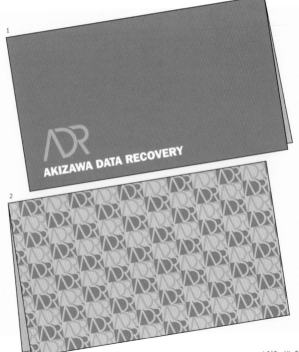

1-3 | *What a difference dimensions can make! How about a fold-over business card?*

The front of this design [1] features the company's name and logo; the back [2] is filled with a decorative pattern built from the company's monogram; and the inside [3] contains a repeat of the monogram along with a slogan and the required corporate info. A person who receives a card such as this is treated to a fresh visual discovery every time they unfold or turn over one of its panels.

When fonts such as these are applied to austere

3

On-site Data Recovery since 1999

ADR

John H. Smith *Vice President*

1234 56th Avenue Northwest
Suite #4061
Seattle, Washington 98225

Wk: 206.765.4321
Cel: 206.123.4567

john@akizawadata.com

AKIZAWADATA.COM

The response card featured below is a good example of a project where usability trumps thematic flourish. Use the design alternatives featured on this spread to explore options when presenting information such as this in a user-friendly way.

1,2 | *Should your type be in line with the linework [3] or sitting above it [2]?*
If your upper and lowercase type is positioned above the linework, make sure that its descenders either avoid—or neatly intersect with—the lines below. (Hint: this issue

can be avoided by using all-caps.)

3 | A confusing relationship between the type and linework exists in this layout—it's not clear whether the form's user is supposed to write on the line above or below each

layouts, their effect is similar to that of a taste-

```
1
```

Yes, please send me more information.

First name: _____ Last name: _____

Company (opt.): _____

Street: _____ Apt/Suite #: _____

City: _____ State/Province: _____

Zip/Postal code: _____ Country: _____

Phone: (____)_____

This is a ☐ *work* ☐ *home phone number (please check one).*

Email (opt.): _____

```
2
```

First name: _____

Company (opt.): _____

Street: _____

City: _____

```
3
```

First name: _____ 🚫

Company (opt.): _____

Street: _____

City: _____

label. Avoid these user-unfriendly mistakes!

4 | Type can rest right on a line if it is bold enough to keep lower portions of letters such as **E** and **L** from disappearing into the linework.

5 | *How about reversing your type out of small background panels?*

6 | Consider using dots, dashes or hand-drawn rules instead of lines.

7 | Guide-boxes can help ensure that a form is filled out neatly and legibly.

8,9 | *How about defining informational areas by using linework or panels?*

fully decorated silk tie or a pair of hipster

4

FIRST NAME:

COMPANY (OPT.):

STREET:

CITY:

5

FIRST NAME:

COMPANY (OPT.):

STREET:

CITY:

6

First name:

Company (opt.):

Street:

City:

7

FIRST NAME

COMPANY (OPT)

STREET

CITY

8

FIRST NAME:

COMPANY (OPT.):

STREET:

CITY:

9

FIRST NAME:

COMPANY (OPT.):

STREET:

CITY:

This spread and the next offer idea-fuel for ways of presenting textually concise information such as this set of photographic classifications (quoted from a book by none other than Ansel Adams).

1 | The scrupulous use of tab stops, different font weights and the use of italics might be all that's needed to bring a clear sense of order to different levels of information within a block of text.

2 | If liberties are allowed with your text, consider the use of subheads and compositional aids (such as this two-column approach) to bring an additional sense of clarity and structure to the information you are presenting.

eyeglasses worn by an otherwise conservativel

1

Portraiture can be classified as follows;

1. The casual or "candid" approach which stresses subject aspects over planned or carefully conceived compositions.

2. The environmental approach which strives to organize the subject together with significant objects, etc.

3. The formal "studio" approach where the subject is stressed together with the elements of personal or conventional style.

2

PORTRAITURE CAN BE CLASSIFIED AS FOLLOWS;

CASUAL 1. The casual or "candid" approach which stresses subject aspects over planned or carefully conceived compositions.

ENVIRONMENTAL 2. The environmental approach which strives to organize the subject together with significant objects, etc.

FORMAL 3. The formal "studio" approach where the subject is stressed together with the elements of personal or conventional style.

The text featured on pages 120-124 is from *Camera and Lens, The Creative Approach*, by Ansel Adams.

1 | Hoefler   2 | Helvetica

3-6 | Linework is a champion of organization. *How about using linework to divide and frame your information?* Explore different weights, configurations, colors and positions for both your linework and the text it supports.

lad businessperson. Keep tabs on media that

3

Portraiture can be classified

1. | The casual or "candid" app
stresses subject aspects o
carefully conceived compo

2. | The environmental approac
to organize the subject tog
significant objects, etc.

3. | The formal "studio" approa
subject is stressed togethe
elements of personal or cor

4

Portraiture can be

1 The casual or "candid"
subject aspects over pl
conceived composition

2 The environmental ap
organize the subject to
objects, etc.

3 The formal "studio" ap
is stressed together with

5

Portraiture can be classified as follows

| **1** | The casual or "candid"
approach which stresses
subject aspects over planned
or carefully conceived com-
positions. | **2** | The envi-
ronmental approach which
strives to organize the subject
together with significant
objects, etc. | **3** | The
formal "studio" approach
where the subject is stressed
together with the elements of
personal or conventional style.

6

*Portraiture can
classified as fol*

The *casual* or "candid" a
which stresses subject as
planned or carefully conc
compositions.

①

The *environmental* appro
strives to organize the su
together with significant ol

②

1 | A computer-like presentation can be used to convey a hyperbolic sense of the absolute. The monospaced font, **>** symbols and a ledger-like background in this layout add implications of cyber-certainty to the design. IF AN APPROACH LIKE

THIS MIGHT SUIT A PROJECT OF YOURS, SEE CHAPTER 5, TECHNOLOGY, FOR MORE IDEAS.

2 | *How about a more casual approach to order? Here, themes of friendliness and order co-exist harmoniously. Compare*

this solution with the one above it—what sort of reader might be drawn to each? Keep the preferences of your target audience in mind when you design! SEE TARGETING AUDIENCE, PAGE 128.

focuses on topics such as finance, medicine, law

1

Portraiture can be classified as follow

> 1. The casual or "candid" approach wh

stresses subject aspects over planned o

carefully conceived compositions.

> 2. The environmental approach which stri

to organize the subject together with

2

Portraiture can be classified as follows

The casual or "candid" approach which stresses subject aspects over planned or carefully conceived compositions.

1.

2.

The environmental approach which strives to organize the subject together with significant objects, etc.

3. The formal "studio" approach where the subject is stressed together with the

1 | Andale Mono   2 | House Gothic

nd science in order to foster your awareness of

3

*ortraiture
can be classified
as follows;*

The casual or "candid" approach which stresses subject
aspects over planned or carefully conceived compositions.

The environmental approach which strives to organize the
subject together with significant objects, etc.

The formal "studio" approach where the subject is stressed
together with the elements of personal or conventional style.

1 | A reminder: A design can "succeed" aesthetically and still fail because of misguided thematic aim. *Varied typefaces, bright colors and skewed panels may amount to a playful and energetic web page design, but will it inspire* confidence on the part of clients who will be investing large amounts of money in an architectural project? Not likely.

2,3 | Balance, harmony, regularity and organization to the rescue. The cleanly structured type and graphic elements within these orderly web page designs do a far better job communicating this company's persona and purpose.

the different shades of order and professionalism that can be generated through type. Call upon the instincts that you have gained through observation and evaluation whenever you are composing layout

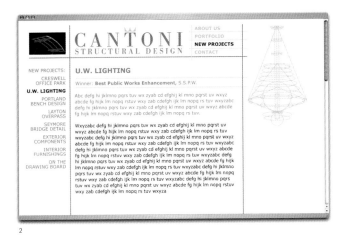

2

directed toward an audience's pragmatic interests.

3

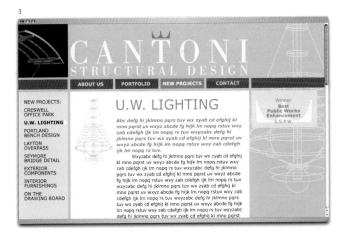

Fonts used in this chapter:

One representative is shown for each typeface family.

SERIF TYPEFACES	SANS SERIF
Berkeley Old Style	Avenir
Bodoni Antiqua	Formata
Bodoni Poster	**Franklin Gothic**
Caslon	Frutiger
Caslon Openface	**Futura**
Century Schoolbook	Gill Sans
Clarendon	Giotto
Didot	Helvetica
ENGRAVERS MT	House Gothic
Hoefler	**Knockout**
Optima	News Gothic
Requiem	Univers
Rockwell	Verdana
Sabon	
Stempel Garamond	

MONOSPACE

Andale Mono

Lucida Sans Typewriter

**SCRIPT, HANDLETTERED
AND CALLIGRAPHIC**

Edwardian Script

Ex Ponto

NOVELTY, DISPLAY

BUZZER THREE

Hollyweird

ORNAMENT FONTS

WebOMints

FOCUS ON:
Targeting Audience

The real distinction between fine and commercial artists (designers included) isn't so much in the art they create as it is in their motivation for creating it. Fine artists are free to promote their personal beliefs or agenda through their images; commercial artists are charged with addressing the wants and needs of their client's target audience through their creations.

No matter what a piece of text says, it can't say it *right* if the *wrong* font is used. And *right*, to a designer, is always that which effectively connects the client's message with the people who are most likely to respond positively to that message. Therefore, if the right fonts, colors, images, concepts and styles of presentation are to be employed, a designer must begin each project with the preferences of this sought-after demographic slice in mind. Consider employing the tactics outlined below as a way of zeroing-in on the identity and tastes of your client's ideal respondent.

Start by asking clients what *they* know about the perfect customer for the ad, brochure, website, etc., that you will be designing for them. What are the members of this target audience like? What *do* these people like? What is their age range? Is it a predominantly male or female group? Conservative or progressive? Sophisticated or simple? Take notes (clients love it when designers take notes)! If your clients do not seem to have clear answers to these questions, work with them to come up with conclusions that everyone is comfortable with. It is important you and your client are in-sync about the identity and characteristics of the target audience for a project before the creative work begins. Agreement concerning these factors can help ensure a streamlined working relationship, since it gives all participants a shared criteria for evaluating your upcoming designs.

Once you have a handle on who the people are that

your design will be targeting, you then need to get a feeling for their taste in fonts, colors, images and styles of design. Look at magazines, advertisements, books, movies and the packaging of the music this group of people favors. You can learn a lot about demographic groups outside your own in this way (sometimes, more than you want to know)—including which kinds of fonts and styles of design seem to resonate with them. Evaluate a broad cross-section of design material. What seems to be working? What doesn't? What looks fresh; what looks stale? Use this kind of media survey for inspiration as well as to get an idea of what you will need to do in order to make your work stand out from competitor's designs that are aimed toward the same segment of the population. Combine audience-targeting strategies such as these with your ever-developing font selection savvy (SEE FONT SELECTION, PAGE 52) to come up with typographic solutions that will agree with the tastes of your client's ideal respondent. Effective designers are those who are able to consistently choose fonts and design approaches that keep the preferences of their audience paramount without sacrificing their own artistic integrity.

Cultivate your font-selection and artistic instincts by keeping your eyes and mind open to what's going on in design (and perhaps more importantly, life itself) throughout the world's cultures and sub-cultures.

> Effective designers are those who are consistently able to choose fonts and design approaches that keep the preferences of their audience paramount without sacrificing their own artistic integrity.

129

Rebellion

Projecting themes of **rebellion, individuality, spontaneity, discord** and **chaos** through type and its supporting compositional elements.

Themes of extreme rebellion are not usually applied directly to letterforms or fonts since chaos tends to run contrary to the first commandment of typography: legibility.

When creating layouts that are meant to deliver rambunctious connotations, designers often preserve the integrity of their typography's readability by calling upon other graphic elements to deliver the thematic portion of their message. Intriguing backdrops, expressive colors, offbeat images and compositional acrobatics could each be employed to lend their thematic projections to nearby typefaces—faces whose own conveyances of disorder might be kept in check for the sake of legibility.

Stephen Hawking, the renowned theoretica

This chapter, therefore, places an extra degree of emphasis on the environment in which type is presented, as well as on custom treatments that can be applied to mar the tidy appearance of letterforms.

Looking for ways to infuse layouts with inferences of individuality, spontaneity, discord or downright chaos? Explore approaches that rely on a chosen typeface to establish the layout's mood; ideas that call upon

non-typographic elements to deliver the piece's conveyances; and solutions that employ both type and non-type elements to contribute to the thematic voice of the design.

physicist, writes, "It is a matter of common

1-6 | *Flip, flop, clip or crop. Polka-dots? How about a splattering of digital paint?* Begin your exploration of disorderly conveyances by bending and breaking the rules of typography—reshaping these rules until they conform to the offbeat conceptual framework of your design.

Ideas as basic as those shown here contain the seeds of far-flung typographic solutions. When aiming for expressions of rebellion, start small, go over the top, and then scale your ideas until they match the visual and conceptual goals you are after.

7 | At the risk of offending the deities of typography (as well as the humans who design fonts), explore the contorting effects of

experience that disorder will tend to increase i

software filters and digital effects. Skew, twist, damage and deform letterforms *en route* to conveyances of individuality and irregularity.

8 | *As opposed to using cyber tools to abuse letterforms, how about defacing* *characters with the help of some real world effects?* Here, a stain from an overloaded coffee cup was photographed and digitally combined with a letterform to give it an all-too-familiar look of wear and tear. What other kinds of damage could you inflict on typographic forms to elicit unruly conveyances? Such effects could be applied to individual letters, whole words, entire paragraphs or full pages of text.

things are left to themselves." *Perhaps this*

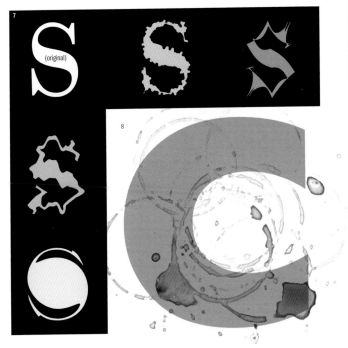

Whether it's a bull or a bullfinch that's let loose in a china shop, disorder is bound to occur on some level. This assertion applies to more than just the well-being of fine dinnerware; refined typographic designs can also be transformed, tarnished or reduced to fragments simply by changing fonts, applying digital effects or destabilizing their compositional structure.

1-9 | The stately monograms from pages 62-63 have been brought to this spread and used as typographic guinea pigs in a demonstration that highlights the narrow separation between themes as (seemingly) far apart as elegance and rebellion. Flip back and forth between this spread

explains why so many of us can relate to visua

1 | Castellar, Kuenstler Script   2 | Dearest, Impact   3 | Futura   4 | Giotto   5 | Bodoni Antiqua, Stencil

and its earlier rendition and take note of the ways in which the previous set of monograms has been treated (mistreated?) to create the designs shown here. *Do any of these transformations spark ideas of how you could amplify tones of*

rebellion in designs of your own?

Looking for new ways of shaking up your typographic compositions? Try using the word list on pages 164-167 to kick-start your brainstorming process.

And remember: The concepts demonstrated throughout this chapter can be applied to all sorts of projects—not just those that are the focus of the particular spread in which they are featured.

onnotations of disorder and rebellion — they are

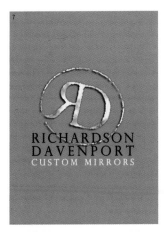

themes that represent an all-too-familiar stat

Univers

Typography need not
play a major role when
it comes to transmitting
a threatening or discom-
forting theme.

f affairs. Untidy themes, in fact, might be far

8.

Painted or photographic portraits that do not hide a person's idiosyncrasies or "flaws" can be much more revealing of their subject's true nature than idyllic representations. Take a look at the "typographic portraits" featured on this spread

and the next. Note how intentional imperfections have been employed in each of these word graphics to help them make revealing statements about their subject.

1 | *Could a digital effect be applied to your set of words to promote a deeper level of meaning? Consider blurring, bending or damaging some or all of the characters in your word group.*

more effective points of connection when dealin

1 | Oculus   2 | Stencil   3 | Python   4 | Helvetica   5 | Clarendon   6 | Klavika

2 | *How about cutting up a typeface or taking it apart at the joints to deliver tumultuous conveyances?*

3 | *A portrait of life in barcode hell? Consider fonts that push legibility to the edge.*

4 | Words can retain a surprising amount of readability when facing backward. Here a conveyance of subtle rebellion is expressed by a single word that defies the status quo.

5 | Graffiti-like additions are ripe with anti-establishment connotations.

6 | The legibility of this type survives in spite of competition from graphic elements that carry messages of both chaos and creativity.

with the population at large than expressions

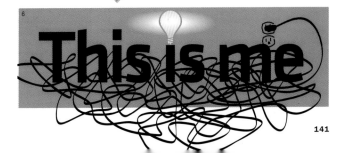

How about incorporating an image in your word graphic?

1 | The treated photo of a broken window used as a backdrop in this typographic portrait would challenge the legibility of any font.

A bold sans serif face might be the only practical option when integrating type with an image that is as chaotic as this.

2 | The old ink blot test: its message depends on the mind of the beholder.

When creating any kind of word graphic, brainstorm for intriguing ways of combining relevant images and revealing text.

3 | Readers might feel a sense of reward and participation when they've

of stability or refinement. Furthermore, t

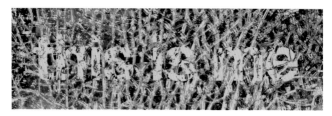

had to contemplate an image (even if only for a moment) to uncover potential meanings.

4 | Look for unorthodox ways of captioning images that convey your design's theme.

5 | *Is there an eye-catching way of digitally altering the letters or words in a photograph to deliver your textual and thematic message?*

6 | In this design, a graceful font playfully leaps strands of dark hair. The type—and its improvised placement— seem to tell us something about what goes on behind the eyes of this model. Try out all kinds of typefaces when combining images and type. Surprising connotations often arise from unlikely choices.

any, disorder is not seen as a negative, but as

When aiming for a visual ambiance that lies outside the realm of mainstream sensibilities, consider design solutions that likewise defy tradition.

1 | Here, connotations of individuality are generated through overlapping characters, varied type sizes, mixed colors and a digitally roughened inline font. These are balanced by the stability implied by the use of a single typeface within the design. *How rebellious do you want your logo to appear? What can be done to amplify or restrain its projections of insubordination?*

2,3 | A short list of treatments and techniques to consider when aiming for non-traditional design solu-

an indication of spontaneity, individualism

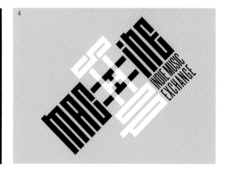

1 | Industria   2 | Knockout, United Stencil   3 | Magda   4 | Thomas, Knockout

tions: Repetition, contemporary color schemes, words obscured by others, untidy fonts, off-center type placement, and backdrops that interfere with legibility.

4 | As long as legibility is not obliterated, it is permissible to challenge readability when thematic goals warrant an out-of-the-ordinary presentation.

5,6 | *How about mixing fonts to achieve a look of funky opposition?*

7 | The letterforms in this design are defined by background panels that convey jaunty messages of their own. Consider counter-intuitive ways of framing type when targeting an offbeat theme.

reativity and real life. Whether you're aiming

A logo may be purely typographic, or it can contain a visual element such as an icon, decoration, photo or illustration. This spread features designs where typography has been integrated directly with a graphic element of some kind. When designing logos, consider avenues of exploration that include images as well as those that don't.

1 | *How about altering a historical image for use in your logo?* Designs such as this might be created in addition to a company's "official" logo for use on promotional items such as posters, stickers or T-shirts.

2 | Use software to bend, morph and combine type with other graphic elements. Keep your goals of theme

to inject unruly connotations into a logo, head

1 | Thomas, Fette Fraktur   2 | Iron Maiden   3 | Thomas

and concept foremost when brainstorming for appropriate effects and image material.

3 | Here, a photo of a sidewalk utility cover makes an effective backdrop for an industrial-strength font.

A suggestion: Use your digital camera to amass your own stockpile of potential backdrop images.

4 | A photo of a manhole cover and a blank CD were digitally combined to form the backdrop for this

design. The font's angular forms connect well with the geometric shapes in the background image. Seek aesthetic connections such as this when searching for ways of establishing a sense of connection between different elements of a design.

ine, paragraph, page or publication, it is only

4

1 | Images and fonts that appear hand-drawn can be employed to add casual notes to a design that might otherwise appear a bit edgy. Here, loosely rendered smoke coming from a zany factory's stacks is complemented by a font that mimics hand-drawn letterforms.

2 | In this design, a matter-of-fact typeface is paired with an icon that carries definite connotations of anarchy. Investigate font/icon pairings that are both complementary and contrasting. Evaluate the results in terms of their aesthetic appeal and their relevance to your thematic goal.

3-5 | When creating a logo, try out a variety of ways of

fitting to rebel against traditional rules o

1 | Big Cheese (factory illustration), Motion   2 | Helvetica

combining your pictorial and typographic elements. Explore different positions, colors and layering choices for the icon or image. Typographically, investigate font, color and structural options. *Should the logo's type come from one font family? Two? Several? How should the type be aligned and scaled? What typographic arrangements interact best with the icon's proportions?*

The more offbeat you wish your logo to appear, the further outside the norm you may have to venture in order to come up with solutions that are satisfactorily radical.

ypography and design — and the degree to

On this spread and the next, sticker designs are used to illustrate a range of conceptually and compositionally offbeat approaches to headline presentation.

1,2 | A black-and-white statement set in a bold,

matter-of-fact font, leaves little doubt as to the conviction behind its rebellious attitude. Capital letters, bloodred coloring and a border-to-border presentation are also powerful carriers of in-your-face conveyances.

3 | The white boxes that are a part of this untidy font form a series of vertical bands when stacked like so. The eye-catching effect is similar to a warning sign or a cut-and-paste ransom note—both of which carry connotations

which you depart from tradition affects th

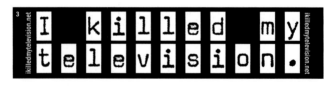

1 | Haettenschweiler, Avenir   2 | Knockout   3 | Magda   4 | Kamaro, Avenir   5 | French Script, Avenir

that are relevant to this design's undertone of social subversion.

4 | *How about using a font that gains notice by virtue of extremes?* Ultra expanded letterforms pack the dimensions of this design with connotations of progressive individuality.

5-7 | Consider using fonts, backdrops, images and colors that put an unexpected spin on your message. Notes of humor, dry wit and irony can be delivered and amplified through fonts and their presentation.

8 | Handy art: Look through image-oriented font families for ready-to-go graphics that enforce the conceptual and visual effects you are targeting.

strength of your anarchical conveyances.

1 | Intentional mayhem. Younger and more progressive audiences tend to have a greater tolerance for difficult-to-read type than older viewers and those with conservative tastes. Magazines, websites and advertisements that are aimed at specific demographic groups are useful resources for designers who are trying to get a handle on a particular group's typographic tastes and tolerances.

2 | *A comic strip? How about showing up for your next client meeting with something completely unexpected? After all, if artists and designers don't smash the status quo of visual communication, who will?*

Typefaces regularly embody themes such a

1 | Myriad Tilt, Helvetica   2 | Helvetica Rounded

3 | Is there an image from the lexicon of pop culture that could be revised in some way to carry the offbeat conveyances of your design? How about replacing a portion of the image with a textual message?

4 | Here, an italic typeface lends conveyances of action and movement as it circles a static "do not" symbol. Never underestimate the range of thematic and aesthetic outcomes that can be generated using readily available fonts, dingbats and symbols (even the funky television at the center of this design was taken from an all-image "font family").

elegance, minimalism, order and simplicity,

3 | Helvetica   4 | Helvetica, Postino, Big Cheese (TV illustration), Webdings ("do not" symbol)

When a radical theme calls for a message that is more than a mere headline, explore ideas that bring fonts, backdrops, images and color schemes together in a compositional free-for-all that honors the message being delivered. The possibilities are infinite.

since these qualities do not inherently interfer

White text: Python   Background text: Kamaro, Knox

with a font's legibility. Rebellion, on the other

(chorus)
Television, the drug of the nation
Breeding ignorance and feeding radiation

T.V. is the place where the pursuit of
happiness has become the pursuit of trivia
where toothpaste and cars
have become sex objects
where imagination is sucked out of children
by a cathode ray nipple
T.V. is the only wet nurse
that would create a cripple
on...

(chorus)
Television, the drug of the nation
Breeding ignorance and feeding radiation

>> Artist: Michael Franti <<
>> Song: Television, the drug of the nation <<
>> Album: Hypocrisy is the greatest luxury, 1991 <<

This spread (and the next) features a series of predominantly typographic poster designs for a contemporary film school.

1 | Consider employing a typeface that delivers both informational *and* thematic content. Here, a stencil face has been used to impart connotations of urban defiance. Its randomly tilted letters and blurred edges (achieved using Photoshop filters) add notes of gritty authenticity to the design.

2 | A font with extreme differences between its condensed and expanded versions, along with a composition that makes use of carefully considered size contrasts, lend a look of calculated rebellion to this layout. Experiment with

hand, is one of those themes that tends to threate

1 | United Stencil, Python (logo, each design)   2 | Kamaro

design solutions that go overboard when seeking radically expressive connotations—you can always tone things down if they get out of hand.

3 | Designs that challenge viewers' interpretation

are admissible if the end result properly reflects the ambiance of the message/organization they represent.

4 | It doesn't take much to impart notes of playful spontaneity to an upright typeface. Here, a straightfor-

ward font is given a hipster twist by framing and outlining its characters with loosely rendered background shapes.

be readability of a typeface—especially if it is

1 | *What kinds of images could be placed beneath your typographic message to add layers of meaning and visual interest? How much background interference can your typeface handle before it loses too much legibility to deliver its message? Here, playful tension is intentionally fostered by combining a straightforward typeface with a set of funky illustrations.*

Note also that standard conventions of capitalization were cast aside when the type was added to this layout. And why not? Why leave rules of grammar alone as long as you are already messing with rules of design?

---

applied with a heavy hand (or fist, as the cas

1 | Franklin Gothic, Big Cheese (all illustrations)

2 | *How about adding a human element to your composition?* The speaking head in this layout adds an animated sense of voice, action and participation to the design.

The disorderly arrangement of the layout's upper elements carry conveyances of spontaneity while the rigid formation of the lower typography establishes a practical undertone for the piece. Tidy compositional structures can be inserted into unruly designs to add notes of restraint and reliability. Allow your artistic inner-voice to tell you when your offbeat design needs taming and when it needs to be stirred to a greater frenzy. If an adjustment to the piece's tone is needed, make typographic and compositional changes accordingly.

nay be). Keep your target audience in mind

When setting text whose message is rebellious in nature (either wholly or vaguely), consider font choices and compositional approaches that are similarly outside the norm.

1 | Images can be added to words to create context and to boost the visual impact of their presentation. Most fans of Patti Smith (or the punk movement in general) are familiar with the white shirt and black suspenders she famously wore for the cover of her album, *Horses.* Here, a rendering of Patti Smith's (in)famous outfit is used as a backdrop for words she spoke during a 1996 interview.*

2 | An image of a gritty sidewalk makes a visually

when creating layouts that embody rambunctiou

1

And, you know, I really think that great art is seductive on various levels. You don't have to be able to understand it. I mean, if you're touched by it or you feel any kind of cerebral response, it's done its work. I couldn't tell you what Pollock meant in "Blue Poles"—it's not necessary. I don't really know what Bob Dylan was talking about in "Desolation Row," but it doesn't really matter. I'm not an analyzing type.

*The text featured on pages 160-164 is from **Woman As Warrior**, by Michael Bracewell, *The Guardian*, June 22, 1996.

intriguing backdrop while generating conveyances of the downtown environment of the artist's heyday performances. A dark halo was added around the type to ensure its readability against the active background.

3 | *How about breaking up your text, thought by thought?* Non-traditional solutions such as this invite reader involvement while delivering connotations of creative nonconformity.

4 | Consider using a variety of fonts within your block of text to give it a unique visual voice. Experiment with typeface combinations between— and within—font families.

hemes—how much legibility-interference will

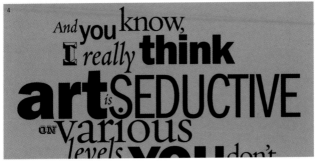

1 | Is there a path other than the straight and narrow that your text could follow? A path with a meaningful conceptual connection with the text's mood or message?

2 | Many of the samples in this section feature relatively standard fonts in chaotic environs. How about switching things around and presenting a zany font within a straightforward composition?

3,4 | What if you applied a digital effect to your entire block of text? Software encourages play and experimentation—it's as easy to save the good ideas as it is to delete the bad ones.

they tolerate? Should a zany typeface be used i

1 | Franklin Gothic   2 | Python   3,4 | Franklin Gothic

If type-altering effects are of interest to you, stay abreast of current technological developments in this area through trade-oriented magazines, books and websites.

5 | For something completely different, explore inventive routes to a finished product. Here, text was laser printed onto a sheet of paper which was then torn, crumpled and photographed. Multimedia, multi-step procedures such as this allow for experimentation and variation during each phase of the creative process.

our layout, or should a straightforward face be

5

And, you know, I really think that great art is seductive on various levels. You don't have to be able to understand it; I mean, if you're touched by it or you feel any kind of cerebral response, it's done its work. I couldn't tell you what Pollock meant in "Blue Poles" - it's not necessary. I don't really know what Bob Dylan was talking about in "Desolation Row," but it doesn't really matter. I'm not an analyzing type.

As the saying goes, rules are meant to be broken. Typographically speaking, this axiom might be expanded to a longer-winded version that reads, "rules are meant to be broken as long as doing so promotes a desired theme without attracting too much attention to the rule breaking itself or interfering excessively with legibility."

accompanied by non-typographic elements tha

Since this chapter deals with themes of rebellion, it's only fitting that its final section differs significantly from the concluding pages of each of the other chapters. Here, instead of offering examples of individual page designs that deliver a particular theme, brainstorming fuel is provided that can be applied to any sort of page design that calls for a look of rebellion. In fact, feel free to apply the prompts presented here to absolutely any kind of project that deals in themes of this genre. This brainstorming aid is offered in the form of a word list (a list that begins on this spread and finishes on the next) that contains a collection of nouns, verbs and adjectives. The words are each related—in some

Large background type: Klavika   Brainstorming list: Giant

way or another—to a concept or treatment that could be applied to typographic or pictorial elements to lend them a measure of thematic angst. Many designers find theme-based lists like this useful when it comes to getting their creative gears engaged and running smoothly toward particular conceptual and visual goals.

deliver the desired level of anarchy to your design?

ADD IMAGE

BACKWARD

BEND

BLUR

BURN

COLLAGE

COLLAPSE

COLLIDE

CONTRAST

CORRODE

CRACK

CROP

CROWD

CRUMPLE

CUT AND PASTE

DAMAGE

DEFORM

DIGITAL EFFECTS

DISCOLOR

DISTORT

FADE

FILL

FRAGMENT
FRAME
GHOST
GRAFFITI
GRAPHIC ELEMENT
LABEL
LAYER
LINEWORK
LINK
MISALIGN
MIX COLORS
MIX FONTS
MIX SIZES
MOTION
NEGATIVE
NONSENSE
OUTLINE
OVERFLOW

OVERLAP
PERSPECTIVE
REARRANGE
REVERSE
RUST
SCATTER
SIDEWAYS
SILHOUETTE
SPIRAL
SPLATTER
SPLIT
STAMP
STENCIL
TWIST
UPSIDE DOWN
WRINKLE
YELL
ZIGZAG

There are relatively few ways to build an automobile that will find wide acceptance in the marketplace at any given time; there will always be countless ways of modifying, damaging or destroying those automobiles—as statistics can easily verify. What does this have to do with typography and design? Just this: destruction, disorder and rebellion are relatively easy themes to generate—easier, by far, than themes such as order and refinement, which have to conform to tighter tolerances of acceptability. This is good news for designers and typographers who are working on projects that call for some degree of thematic degeneration: the possibilities are truly endless.

167

Fonts used in this chapter:

One representative is shown for each typeface family.

SERIF TYPEFACES

Bodoni Antiqua

CASTELLAR

Clarendon

PERPETUA

Postino

Requiem

Wide Latin

SANS SERIF

Avenir

Briem Akademi

Franklin Gothic

Futura

Gill Sans

Giotto

Haettenschweiler

Helvetica

Helvetica Rounded

House Gothic

Impact

Industria

Klavika

Knockout

Univers

**SCRIPT, HANDLETTERED
AND CALLIGRAPHIC**

Dearest

Edwardian Script

Fette Fraktur

French Script

Kuenstler Script

Zapfino

NOVELTY, DISPLAY

GIANT

IRON MAIDEN

Kamaro

KNOX

Magda

Motion

Myriad Tilt

Oculus

PA+RI⊕+

Python

STENCIL

thomas

UNITED STENCIL

ORNAMENT FONTS
Big Cheese
Webdings
Wingdings

FOCUS ON:

Visual Hierarchy

Along with attaining aesthetic objectives, composition's *raison d'être* is to lead the viewer's eye through a layout's various elements in a helpful manner. In most cases, this visual progression begins with the carrier of the piece's primary message and moves on to elements that provide additional thematic support and factual information.

Author's note: When writing about design fundamentals, visual hierarchy is one topic that I can't fathom leaving out. Therefore, I include this note for two purposes: first to apologize for featuring this subject for the third time in as many books; and second, to promise readers who have heard from me on this topic before that I've made every effort to look at it from a fresh angle this time around—with special emphasis on particulars related to typography.

of a design. When creating a layout that is meant to attract attention, it is usually best to place one element clearly at the top of the visual hierarchy totem pole (a position that is often given to a headline or featured image). This element acts as the point of entry into the layout—a lure that snares attention, rouses interest and incites the viewer to further investigate the layout and its message.

Likewise, supporting elements of a design ought* to be present-

Use your knowledge of design and composition to direct an appropriate degree of

HIERARCHY = RANK; ORDER OF IMPORTANCE. **Visual hierarchy** is a term that refers to the different levels of apparent status that have been given to each element

ed in a way that denotes their individual importance as they support and expand upon the layout's thematic and literal messages. This sense of rank among a layout's elements is achieved by adjusting aesthetic variables in regard to size, visual weight, position, color and tint. Use your knowledge of design and composition to direct an appropriate degree of attention to each element of your layout's components (and to establish clear distinctions between the visual rank of each).

In terms of boosting the visual status of a typographic element within a layout, consider using one or more of the following methods: increase the size of the font; use a bolder weight; add empty space around the type element; backdrop; switch to a font that demands more notice by virtue of novel or eye-catching qualities.

Conversely, the visual impact of a typographic element can be lessened by applying the above-mentioned techniques in reverse.

And remember, typographic elements are not the only factors in the visual hierarchy equation. The aesthetic and conceptual impact of photographs, illustrations, graphic elements, backdrops, borders and colors should also be taken into account as you construct and finalize a layout.

Learn from the masters: The next time you look at a Renaissance masterpiece, take note of how its composition leads your eye into— and throughout—the painting's environs. You might easily learn a trick or two that could be applied to your design work.

ttention to each of your layout's components.

use other graphic components to frame or point toward the key typographic element; present the type in a stronger hue; place it against a contrasting

*There are definite cases when the absence of visual hierarchy actually promotes a design's goals, i.e., designs that are meant to frustrate viewers appear intentionally bland or deliver strong conveyances of chaos.

CHAPTER 5

Technology

Projecting themes of **technology, futurism, science** and **cyber-reality** through type and its supporting compositional elements.

1 | In all forms of art (typography included), futurism is often expressed through a rethinking and paring down of traditional rules and concepts. Compare the tried-and-true sans serif **g** on the left (Helvetica) with the modern sans serif character to its right (Reykjavik). The newer letterform has given up a measure of grace in exchange for a look of essential simplicity that carries connotations of logical modernity. Forward-thinking typefaces such as this make good candidates for designs that are meant to deliver progressive connotations.

2-8 | In order to generate more exaggerated conveyances of technology and science, certain fonts

Sometimes technology leaps and sometimes ⋯

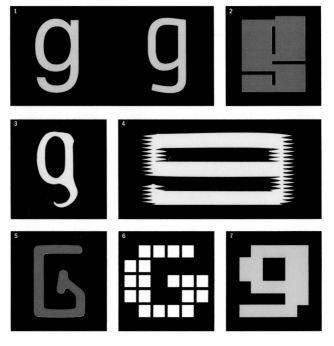

1 | Helvetica, Reykjavik   2 | Thomas   3 | Oculus   4 | Kamaro   5 | Buzzer Three   6 | Genetrix   7 | Joystik

are designed using highly geometric structures; letters that appear distorted by the effects of light; and characters that mimic the ways that letterforms are displayed through electronic media. A wide spectrum of expression is available within this genre—from serious to silly, realistic to whimsical.

rawls. It's rare, however, when the forward

8

1 | Themes and moods can be projected onto typographic elements through visual association. Here, an ambiguously futuristic backdrop lends its connotations of the cyber world to a utilitarian typeface. Frill-free sans serif fonts are particularly capable of absorbing the thematic projections of their environs.

2 | Letterforms from yesteryear can be used as the basis for designs that deliver progressive conveyances.

The condensed serif type in this modernistic logo is from a family of letters that has been around since the days of the steam engine. The first letter of the company's name has been repeated and rotated to form a

momentum of science holds still for long

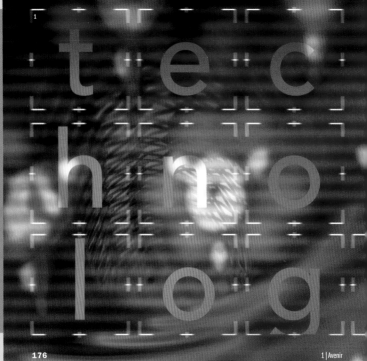

futuristic icon that reflects the logotype's literal meaning.

3-5 | In this example, a letterform that already carries connotations of technology is used as a component in an icon

that delivers amplified projections of modernity [**3**].

Once you come up with an icon design you like, use the computer to experiment with variations such as these dimensional treatments [**4, 5**]. And while you're in

this exploratory mode, try out different arrangements for the typographic elements that accompany the icon: investigate icon/type compositions that are vertical, horizontal, circular and square.

ccordingly, fonts that deliver conveyances of

Could your typographic icon be used as the basis for an intriguing pattern? Patterns such as these can be used as eye-catching and theme-setting elements in all sorts of projects. (PAGES 70-71 FEATURE MORE PATTERNS OF THIS KIND.)

science and technology belong to a genre that is in

ate of constant evolution. Keep tabs on the latest

1-4 | *What about creating your own letterforms from scratch—characters that could be used as a graphic element in a logo or layout? The simple geometric lines and shapes used to create these four letters lend themselves well to* themes of technology and science. *What sorts of design parameters could you apply to a set of letterforms to connect them with a particular theme you are working toward?*

offerings of type foundries that specialize i.

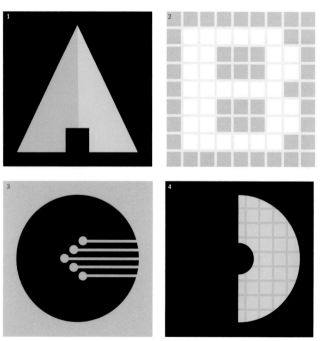

1-4 | custom-drawn characters

5-7 | *How about **capturing** letters or numbers instead of **creating** them?* Use your camera to record intriguing images of electronically rendered and illuminated typographic characters. Images such as these could be cropped, colored and digitally enhanced for use in design projects that call for connotations of modernity.

orward-thinking designs. New typographic

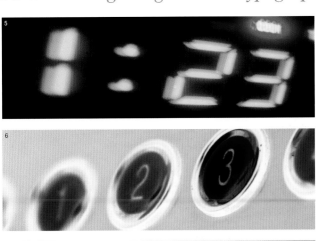

1-4 | Science and technology have a visual vernacular of their own. Certain kinds of numerical arrangements, scientific symbols and descriptive diagrams deliver clear connotations of technology. Note how the exponent-like placement of the **3** in the first design gives this monogram a logical feel. The faux atomic schematic of the next composition [2] lends physics-oriented conveyances to this monogram. The red plus-sign in this monogram [3] is doubly effective since it carries conveyances of both science and medicine. The final set of monograms [4] demonstrates the use of various data-related characters for separating initials.

territory is constantly being explored, mapped an

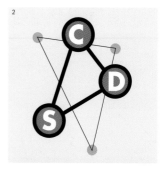

1 | House Gothic   2 | Futura   3 | Kamaro   4 | Methodic

5,6 | *Is there a way of incorporating geometric forms, dimension or perspective into your monogram to infuse it with conveyances of modern (or old-school) sciences?*

7 | The linking letterforms used to build this monogram are well suited as representatives for a company that deals in issues of connectivity. Consider a variety of font choices for your hi-tech typographic design—look for a typeface that has been created around the same thematic conveyances you are seeking for your monogram or logo design.

onquered by innovative designers worldwide.

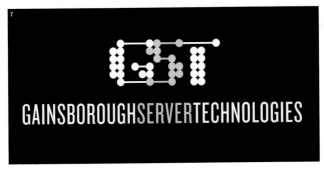

5 | Univers   6 | Bionika   7 | Python, Knockout

Consider applying digital effects to type in order to convey technologically related messages such as... the effect of digital effects.

1 | In this example, a relatively straightforward monogram has been given a work-over in Photoshop to lend it a cyber-punk feel.

The font used for the monogram is from the same family as the type used for the company's name. It is not mandatory to use the same typeface throughout a logo design, but it is a reliable way of establishing underlying connotations of harmony.

Cyber-stylish typefaces are often used in medi

Digital FX
DESIGN STUDIO

2 | Ease-of-exploration is probably technology's greatest gift to designers. It only takes a few minutes to investigate a full range of digital effects using a feature-rich program such as Photoshop. Apply a variety of filters, transformations and colors and save each appealing solution that you come up with. Evaluate your collected favorites based on the visual and thematic goals you are aiming for.

imed toward younger, tech-savvy buyers of

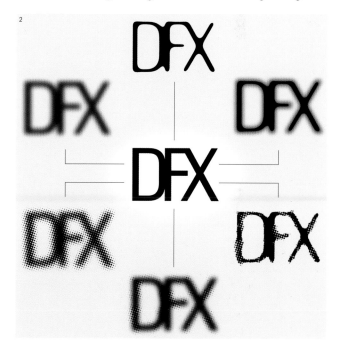

2

1 | *What about creating a graphic that is a literal expression of your hi-tech word or words? Here, 1,024 squares are used to form the backdrop for the word kilobyte. (In spite of the implication of its name, a kilobyte* represents the number 1,024, not 1,000).

2-4 | Type can be used to adorn or caption an image that illustrates the meaning of a word. Explore different font choices for solutions such as these. *Should the* typeface amplify the thematic look-and-feel of the image? Should it be relatively neutral and allow the image to set the tone? Should the typeface contradict the apparent message of the image for purposes of humor or sarcasm?

modern gadgets. Still, it's important to remembe

1 | House Gothic 2 | Formata 3 | Avenir

5,6 | When creating a word graphic, consider solutions that use a typeface whose design reflects the meaning of the word, as well as solutions that rely on digital treatments to give your font the right thematic look. The first sample in this pair features a typeface that is designed to appear as though it is in a state of activity. The second sample features ordinary type that has been exposed to Photoshop's WIND filter to give it a sense of motion.

7 | Be on the lookout for fonts that have a conceptual connection with the word you are treating. The font used for the portrayal of this particular word seems ideal since its **t**s happen to look like plus signs.

that tech-related themes are not always best served

The font you choose for a word graphic or headline can put a definite spin on the text's literal and thematic message. Note the wide range of connotations that arise from the different fonts used for these samples— conveyances ranging from modern to classical, hi-tech to humanistic, scientific to childlike. Never underestimate the influence that a font's visual voice can have on the perceived mood and meaning of a textual message.

by cutting-edge fonts. Take, for example, typeface

1

discovery

2

discovery

3

Discovery

1 | Klavika   2 | Python   3 | Spaceage

rsed in media directed at the upper-level software

4

discovery

5

discovery

6

DISCOVERY

When creating a logotype, consider customizing letters (or words) in ways that emphasize the thematic and/or literal message of the company's name. Use these before-and-after comparisons to help brainstorm for ideas.

1 | Here, the logotype has been streamlined by connecting selected upper serifs with adjacent letterforms. The **f** and second **i** have also been joined to clean up their previously awkward juncture.

2 | In order to assure clear legibility for this logotype, certain letters have been modified: Crossbars have been added to the **f**, and connections between certain letters have been broken in order to establish clearer distinctions between them.

engineers who oversee the design of modern gadgetr

1

infinium   *infinium*

2

infinium   infinium

3

INFINIUM   INFINIUM

4

INFINIUM   **INFIN**IUM

1 | Bodoni Antiqua   2 | Transaxle   3 | Futura   4 | Franklin Gothic

3 | Could certain pairs of your logotype's letters be joined without defeating the word's legibility?

4 | What about a theme-based solution that involves simple variations among your character's weights?

5-7 | Explore ideas that involve graphic additions to—or within—the letterforms of your logotype.

8 | Are there ways of integrating other (perhaps more complex) graphic forms into your logo's design?

Note that this logo carries connotations of both the past and the future through its combination of an aged-looking font and a modern compositional structure.

Media aimed toward this demographic slice often

5

6

7

8

When adding type to an icon, explore a variety of typographic, compositional and coloring options. Maintain an awareness of how these factors are affecting the visual and thematic impact of the logo as a whole.

1 | Here, a font that delivers exaggerated expressions of modernity has been chosen to support a somewhat whimsical graphic element. Contrasting stylistic and proportional characteristics between the logotype and illustration generate offbeat conveyances without defeating the logo's futuristic appeal. A straightforward sans-serif font has been used for the logo's subtext to give the design a sensible undertone.

feature fonts with strong conveyances of logic an.

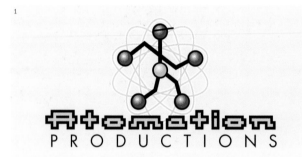

1 | Atomic, Futura   2 | Iron Maiden, Python

2 | *Is there a way of inserting your image directly into the company's name without compromising the type's readability?* Note how the color used inside the type's letterforms matches a color used in the illustration. This color connection helps establish a visual link between the logo's type and icon.

3 | The large separation between the words in this layout might be a compositional liability were it not for a backdrop of lines that fill the design's empty spaces and form a visual link between its various elements. Consider using linework or background panels to establish a pleasing overall shape for your logo and to create a sense of unity among its components.

cademia. The importance of Knowing Thy Audience

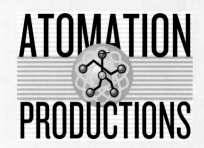

1 | *How about a compart-mentalized approach?* Select a font that fits the proportional requirements and thematic goals of your constructed composition.

2 | The distinctly old-style font used in this progressive design adds a quirky sense of rebellion to the whole. *How about employing a far-fetched font choice to add impertinent undercurrents to the main theme of your logo?*

3 | Typographic heresy or a sign of the times? Here, the quirkiness of the preceding design is further heightened by inserting a most unusual font: a bitmapped version of a centuries-old blackletter font. Keep tabs on the work of contemporary type

(and understanding their typographic and stylist.

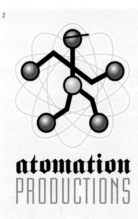

1 | Macroscopic   2 | Fette Fraktur, Briem Akademi   3 | Dotic, Briem Akademi

designers—you never know what kind of outlandish creations they'll come up with.

4,5 Try out compositional solutions that follow the contour of your logo's graphic image—both exactly and not-so-exactly.

6,7 These two logo designs are presented side by side to demonstrate a simple point: Technology is a compliant theme—one that seems to adapt itself equally well to conveyances as far apart as order [6] and

upheaval [7]. Investigate all sorts of conceptual and compositional approaches as you brainstorm, sketch and computer-generate the beginnings of your logo's hi-tech design.

references) is especially relevant when it comes to

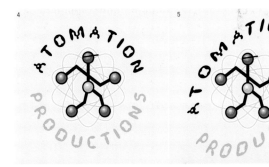

Here, newsletter mastheads are used to demonstrate a series of headline/subhead treatments. Since the newsletter's title has two subheads, additional typographic challenges and possibilities are presented.

1 | *How about incorporating a graphic add-on that enforces the headline's meaning without calling an undue amount of attention to itself?*

2 | The linework and arrow in this design serve two purposes: to separate different textual elements, and to provide a theme-boosting point of interaction with one of the headline's characters.

3,4 | Consider adding graphic elements to—or behind—your headline font.

targeting messages to a specific segment within th

Explore both traditional and non-traditional placements and positions for subheads and other supporting textual elements.

5 | Here, a futuristic font has been used for the headline—a font that does not require help from graphic elements to deliver connotations of technology.

The simple sans serif face used for the subheads adds a grounding influence to the strong personality of the headline font.

6 | Have you considered creating a cohesive design unit for use as a masthead or headline? Panels, color, linework, graphics and images could be employed to build a self-contained compositional structure.

i-tech crowd. Technological and futuristic themes

4

5

6

1 | Play with your type. *Is there a way of delivering all of your progressive conveyances using only typographic elements?*

2 | Consider solutions that defy logic *en route* to a logical looking design.

Here, a single size of type has been used for each of the typographic elements in the masthead design. The newsletter's name is highlighted only by its bright color and slightly heavier weight.

3,4 | Think vertical. Layouts can be built around headlines that occupy a vertical column rather than a horizontal portion of the composition. The upward momentum of the type in the second example **[4]** connects thematically with

can also be expressed in more archetypal terms (

1

Monthly Journal of Interstellar Satellite Guidance System Design

Trajectories

Volume Number 08 ▪ Published by the Multinational Association of Rocket Scientists

2

Monthly Journal of Interstellar Satellite Guidance
System Design > **Trajectories** > Volume 08 > Published
by the Multinational Association of Rocket Scientists

1 | Joystik, Univers   2 | Lucida Sans Typewriter

the meaning behind the newsletter's name. Look for conceptual associations such as this when you design.

5,6 | In general, it is considered a typographic no-no to stack type in this fashion—whether the letters are upper-and-lowercase or all caps. Legibility suffers terribly when type is thus stacked. In most cases, it's preferable to stand type on its side (as in the previous sample) when a vertical orientation is being sought for a type element.

THREE OF THE MASTHEADS FEATURED IN THIS SECTION ARE USED AS ELEMENTS IN PAGE LAYOUT DEMONSTRATIONS ON PAGES 208-209.

ndeed archetypes can arise in a half-century or less).

3
Trajectories

Monthly Journal of Interstallar Satellite Guidance System Design

Vol. 08

Published by the Mulitnational Association of Rocket Scientists

4
Trajectories

5
Monthly Journal of Interstellar Satellite Guidance System Design

Vol. 08

Published by the Multinational Association of Rocket Scientists

5
T r a j e c t o r i e s

6
T R A J E C T O R I E S

In the other chapters of this book, the "Typographic Assemblages" subsection is devoted to demonstrating various ways of *creating* all-type compositions. A different tact has been taken here: ideas are offered to help brainstorm for different ways of *presenting* already-established typographic compositions.

1 | The completed all-type layout for a tech-related conference. This design could be used as is, or it could be integrated into a layout that furthers its thematic expression—as demonstrated in the eight samples that follow.

2 | The logo's shield is used to spawn a sequence of colorful echoes throughout the environs of this design.

Examples: fonts based on the pixilated forms seen o

All designs | Klavika, Bionika (logo)

Conveyances of computer-generated modernity are delivered by the resulting sense of perspective and expansion.

3 | Here, the type has been given a schematic quality by converting it to outlines.

Then, a spiraling wireframe effect was generated to bolster the scientific and exploratory connotations of the design.

4 | Use technology to convey technology. *How about taking a photograph of your design while it is displayed on a computer monitor? Or, what if you used a projector to cast your design's image onto an interesting surface and then took a picture of it?*

nany pre-Macintosh computer monitors; letterforms

1 | This effect was created by exporting the original design into Photoshop where LIGHTING EFFECTS and LENS FLARE filters were applied—a very simple route to a dramatic makeover.

2 | Create or purchase images that could be used as a theme-boosting backdrop. Here, a colorful photograph of arcing tracers of light sits beneath a translucent layer of binary numbers (the foundation of computer language). The result is a dynamic and thematically relevant background for the design's textual message.

3 | *Is there some empty space in your design where an eye-catching photo or two could be inserted?*

that mimic L.E.D. readouts and other light-based

4 | *What about making your typographic assemblage part of a larger image?* Here, a robotic figure takes center stage and seems to be sharing the conference's message by way of cyber-telepathy.

5 | The digitally altered image of a robotic figure peers from behind a layer of translucent type in this design. Both the image and the type were treated and then combined in Photoshop. Explore layering, filtering and translucency effects that push your typographic design into new creative territory.

displays; fonts that bring back "nostalgic" memories

Poetry meets science in this monologue (delivered by an android whose batteries are about to run out) from the 1982 movie, *Blade Runner.**

1 | There are many intriguing fonts that deliver overt conveyances of computer technology. These typefaces might not be the best choice for extended blocks of text (since they are not always the easiest to read) but they are worth considering for shorter excerpts such as this.

of the late 20th century (such as the dot-matrix typ

1

I've seen things you people wouldn't believe. Attack ships on fire off the shoulder of Orion. I watched C-beams glitter in the dark near the Tannhauser gate. All those moments will be lost in time, like tears in rain. Time to die.

*Trivia bytes: In 2004, *The Guardian* (UK) surveyed 60 scientists to find out what they thought was the best science fiction movie of all time. Ridley Scott's *Blade Runner* was their first choice, with Stanley Kubrick's *2001: A Space Odyssey* a close second. The quotation featured in this section—often referred to as the "tears in rain" speech—is considered by many science fiction aficionados to be the penultimate monologue of the movie (if not the entire genre). Hampton Fancher and David Peoples created Blade Runner's screenplay based (loosely) on the 1968 novel by Philip K. Dick, *Do Androids Dream of Electric Sheep?* However, it was Rutger Hauer— the actor who played the leading android in the movie—who spontaneously improvised most of this soliloquy, including the famous line, "all those moments will be lost in time, like tears in rain."

1 | Python

2 | Here, homage is paid to the quotation's poetic *and* technological heritages as the graceful forms of a refined serif font are set above a digitally-inspired backdrop.

3 | The use of underscores between words and the hyphen-free justification of the text in this sample mimic ultra-logical conventions that might be expected of authentic cyber speak (perhaps this is how the quotation would be transcribed if it had actually been spoken by an android). Consider solutions whose thematic honesty compensates for any grammatical mischief.

seen on printed spreadsheets, circa 1970); and even

2

I've seen things you people wouldn't believe. Attack ships on fire off the shoulder of Orion. I watched C-beams glitter in the dark near the Tannhauser gate. All those moments will be lost in time, like tears in rain. Time to die.

3

```
I've_seen_things_you_people_woul
dn't_believe_Attack_ships_on_fire
_off_the_shoulder_of_Orion_I_wat
ched_C-beams_glitter_in_the_dark
_near_the_Tannhauser_gate_All_t
hose_moments_will_be_lost_in_ti
me_like_tears_in_rain_Time_to_di
e
```

No doubt, you've noticed the digitally-rendered characters in the background of this spread (and the one before). Type and color are all it takes to create a mood-setting backdrop.

1 | *Technology never ceases to challenge convention—so why not rise up against typographic conventions when aiming for conveyances of technology? For example, why not begin a paragraph with* a bitmapped all-caps font and allow it to gradually give way to an elegant italic serif to convey the possible connection between circuitry and emotion?

fonts that are more representative of yesteryear's

2 | And remember: If you'd
rather not use a digitally-
inspired font for your text,
but still want to present
your message in a hi-tech
environment, consider
using a "regular" font and
letting other elements of
your design set the com-

position's tone. Here, a
bitmapped set of eyes
peer out from behind the
conceptually neutral forms
of a sans serif typeface.

ence fiction than today's scientific facts.

1

I'VE SEEN THINGS YOU PEOPLE WOULDN'T
BELIEVE. ATTACK SHIPS ON FIRE OFF THE
SHOULDER OF ORION. I WATCHED C-BEAMS
GLITTER IN THE dARK NEAR THE TANNhAUSER
GATE. All THOSE MOMENTS WILL BE LOST IN
TIME, LIKE tears IN rain. Time to die.

2

I've seen things you people wouldn't believe.
Attack ships on fire off the shoulder of Orion.
I watched C-beams glitter in the dark near
the Tannhauser gate. All those moments will
be lost in time, like tears in rain. Time to die.

To bolster a sense of unity throughout your full-page design, seek visual and conceptual echoes between typographic and structural elements of the composition. These echoes could take the form of colors that work well together; typefaces that come from the same family (or complementary families) and logical alignments between various elements of the design.

MASTHEAD DESIGNS HAVE BEEN BORROWED FROM PAGES 196-199 FOR USE IN THE DEMONSTRATIONS SHOWN ON THIS SPREAD.

Designers should not be surprised to find that technology is a theme that can be expressed in all kinds of ways through type—after all, computers and technology are themselves integral components in th

The modernistic font used in this newsletter's masthead sets a progressive tone for the design. A font with better legibility was chosen for the newsletter's articles. To establish a sense of connection between the layout's masthead and content area, a large capital letter was placed at the beginning of the text. This capital comes from the same font as the newsletter's heading and is colored with hues borrowed from the masthead. Additional layout harmony is achieved by applying this color to the divider-lines in the content area.

1

Visual echoes between the masthead and content area of this layout exist in the form of a grid that appears in both portions of the design—and in the rounded corners of the boxes that define the two sections. A typographic echo also exists: the font that is employed as the masthead's subhead is also used for the articles' headlines (same font size, different color). A common color palette used throughout the layout also helps project a unified feel.

2

reation, presentation and evolution of type.

Here, the position of the newsletter's title within the masthead provides a cue for the alignment of the columns below (indicated by the dotted line). Such alignments are yet another way of establishing a sense of connection between various elements of a layout. Further masthead/content unity is conveyed through the use of textual headlines that are set in the same font that appears throughout the masthead. Note also that the white line that divides text blocks in the content area matches the white lines in the masthead. And once again, color is used in this layout to establish a visual tie-in between the masthead and the content area.

3

Fonts used in this chapter:

One representative is shown for each typeface family.

SERIF TYPEFACES

Bodoni Antiqua

Caslon Antique

CASTELLAR

Sabon

Requiem

SANS SERIF

Avenir

Briem Akademi

Formata

Franklin Gothic

Futura

Giotto

Helvetica

House Gothic

Klavika

Knockout

Reykjavik

Univers

MONOSPACE

Andale Mono

Lucida Sans Typewriter

SCRIPT, HANDLETTERED AND CALLIGRAPHIC

Dearest

Fette Fraktur

Motion

NOVELTY, DISPLAY

Atomic

Bionika

BUZZER THREE

Dotic

GENETRIX

IRON MAIDEN

JoyStik

Kamaro

MACROSCOPIC

METHODIC

Oculus

PA+RI⊕+

Python

spaceage

thomas

Transaxle

W1RED

FOCUS ON:
Combining Fonts

Combining typefaces requires a kind of contradictory logic—that of being able to identify typographic connections that are simultaneously *contrasting* and *complementary*. It's a process not unlike finding the right mix of people to perform a musical duet or trio that requires a range of unique voices (baritone, tenor, soprano, etc.) that blend harmoniously as a whole.

One way to promote design harmony within a layout is to use typefaces that come from the same font family. For example, an ad's headline could be set in a bold version of a particular font; the subhead using that font's italics; and the ad's text in the font's regular weight. Naturally, the chosen font's stylistic projections will have a large impact on the look-and-feel of a layout whose type comes from a single extended family—especially if it is an all-type composition.

There are many times, however, when a designer wants to create a layout that expresses itself through more than one font's visual voice. In these cases, different fonts can be assigned to play different thematic and compositional roles. An example of this is when an expressive, high energy font is selected for a headline while a more passive and readable typeface is assigned for roles such as subhead and body text.

There is no exact way of knowing when a layout should feature typefaces from more than one family. Nor is there an exact way of knowing which fonts to combine when multiple typefaces are used. These decisions rely on the designer's instinct—an instinct which arises from time spent learning typographic fundamentals, observing the work of successful designers, and applying one's current typographic knowledge to projects of all kinds and evaluating the results.

The following assortment of thoughts and examples are offered as ideas-to-ponder for readers who are still striving toward a sense of confidence in their font-pairing abilities and instincts.

COMBINING
TYPEFACES

Be decisive when mixing fonts. Combine typefaces that are clearly different from each other. And, at the same time, ask yourself, does it make sense that the visual voices of these particular fonts are speaking together? Do their different characteristics amount to a unified thematic message, ie., professionalism, boldness, elegance, dissension, chaos? Are the fonts meant to be speaking together harmoniously or contentiously? Do the typefaces come from similar societal or historical backgrounds? *Should* they share similar backgrounds?

Consider these factors whenever you combine typefaces—whether you are working on a two-font logo or a multi-font page layout.

It's best to avoid pairing typefaces that are similar in weight and size or fonts that seem to be saying the same thing in slightly different dialects (as with the association of the two nearly-alike stencil faces at bottom). Such combos tend to project conveyances of indecision or tepid compromise. The viewer of these type mixes may wonder if the designer couldn't make up their mind as to which font to use or if a mistake was made in the creation of the artwork.

More samples on the following spread...

213

Fonts with more radical differences between them can be combined to generate elevated expressions of exuberance, quirkiness, dissension or rebellion.

In addition to deciding what fonts to combine in a typographic composition, think about different ways of amplifying connections or differences between the words themselves through color or compositional means. Could color be used to bolster conveyances of harmony or contrast between the two (or more) fonts? How about using wide letterspacing for one word and tightly packing the other to accentuate differences between them? And what about curving the baseline or one word or orienting it vertically?

214

More points and ideas to consider regarding multi-font combos:

Many experienced designers rarely use more than two (or possibly three) fonts within a layout. Exceptions arise when they are aiming for themes that are expansive, celebratory, offbeat or irrational. When in doubt, it's usually best to err on the side using too few— rather than too many—fonts in a layout.

When creating a layout that includes a logo, take the logo's typeface into account when choosing fonts for the rest of the design. Could you use fonts that come from the same family as the logo's type? Would it be better to use typefaces that amicably differentiate themselves from the font(s) used in the logo? If the logo's type comes from a font that is difficult to pair with others, consider allocating some empty space around the logo to lessen the dissension that might otherwise occur between it and other nearby type elements.

The computer gives designers unprecedented freedom to explore the thematic and visual effects of different font combinations. Try out a variety of combos en route to choosing a favorite. Take a look at single-font-family solutions as well as multi-family combinations. Explore pairings that seem logical as well as those that are long-shots—it only takes a moment to pull down a font menu, click on a typeface and view the results (and it's even easier to UNDO your selection if you don't like the results).

Look at the work of accomplished designers. What fonts do they combine within layouts? Note the effects of font pairings that result in a subtle deepening of a layout's sophistication as well as typeface combos that result in radical visual and thematic expressions.

CHAPTER 6

Organic

Projecting themes of **nature, horticulture, humanity** and the **environment** through type and its supporting compositional elements.

1 | The word *organic* is used in this chapter to describe thematic and aesthetic qualities that bear some connection to the natural world and its inhabitants. In this sample, the connection occurs in the form of a letter that

looks as though it were penned onto a sheet of handmade paper, or as if it has been subjected to the effects of weather or age.

2-4 | Letterforms that convey a non-mechanical look of spontaneity are also

featured throughout this section. This sort of character is often designed as a variation of a standard font.

5 | Gracefully rounded serifs connect fluidly with the linear elements of this letter. Details such as these

Every seed comes up with a different solution fo

project a sense of warmth and friendliness that is beyond the expressive scope of fonts that are built of more angular and abruptly-joined elements.

6-14 | Typefaces that are (or appear to be) hand-

rendered relate well with organic themes because of their obvious connection to humanity. The variety of fonts in this category is nearly as broad as the range of handwriting styles that inspires them.

15-17 | Fonts that express their organic themes in conspicuous terms can be especially useful for use as initial caps or in headlines, word graphics, and logos that are aiming for blatant conveyances of the natural world.

he same puzzle. Organic entities on this particular

1,2 | Text ornaments that express visual references to leaves, vines, flowers and other organic entities can be used both for decoration and to inject nature-oriented conveyances into layouts.

3 | This casually-rendered relative of the preceding ornament projects an amplified sense of natural-ness since it comes from a family of hand-drawn decorations. Ornaments such as this can be combined with similarly

styled fonts when strong connotations of grassroots improvisation are being sought. They can also be inserted into compositions that feature straightfor-ward type in order to add a casual note to the overall design.

planet tend to grow and flow according to thei

4 | Ornaments whose design is not rooted in horticulture-based forms can also emit organic conveyances. The casual structure of the ornament used to build this pattern conveys more than its share of easygoing vibes.

5,6 | Edibles are the subject of several font-based ornament and illustration sets. Consider using ready-to-go images such as these as stand-alone illustrations or as building blocks for patterns.

7-11 | In fact, there are font-based illustration sets that contain loosely-rendered images of just about everything under the sun. The natural style of these kinds of images imparts hints of a human touch to whatever subject matter they portray.

...eed for things like warmth, water and sex.

1-4 | Letterforms can be used as the basis for all kinds of organically-inclined images. How about integrating your illustration with a letter that conveys natural themes of its own? What about adding your nature-based image to a *decidedly non-natural typeface? And what if you combined your illustration with a conceptually neutral letterform? Explore options!*

To the human eye, organic growth sometime

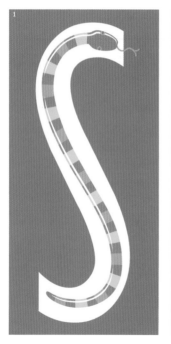

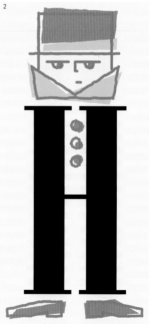

1 | Gill Sans 2 | Bodoni Antiqua

5,6 | Here, connotations of humanity and vision are delivered through illustrations built entirely of typographic characters. Images such as these can link organic themes with conveyances of literature, media and technology.

7 | E-mail has popularized the use of emotion-conveying arrangements of punctuation marks and letters. *Could a typographic "character" such as this make an effective illustration for a non-email project of yours?*

eads to physical forms that are considered

3 | Futura 4 | Critter 5 | Bodoni Antiqua

In addition to leading the viewer's eye to the beginning of text blocks, initial caps also make powerful theme-setting elements.

1 | Many initial caps are designed as ready-to-go organic compositions.

2 | *Looking for an initial cap that expresses itself in more contemporary terms? If so, how about creating one of your own? Here, a lean and geometric letterform has been combined with the custom-drawn, flowing forms of ivy and leaves.*

The result is a unique mix of modernity and tradition.

3 | *Who says that a letter has to be embellished with plant matter in order to convey organic themes? The ladybug that nearly obliterates this capital* **G**

graceful and sensibly structured. Other time

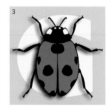

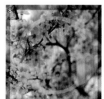

1 | Cloister Initials   2 | Futura, custom-made ornaments   3 | Gill Sans, Insectile   4 | Kamaro, Constructivist Extras

comes from an illustration-based font family that specializes in bugs of all kinds.

4 | This initial cap features a letter that sits atop—rather than being contained within—a set of decorative ornaments. Interestingly,

the laurels used in this layout are from a rather non-organic source: an illustration-based font set of Soviet-era graphics.

5 | *What about doodling your initial cap to convey a truly hand-crafted look?*

6-9 | *How about using a photograph—rather than an illustrated element— to link your custom-made initial cap with an organic theme?* Use software to explore different ways of combining typographic and photographic elements.

rganic forms seem haphazard and difficult to

1 | The handcrafted font used for this monogram projects conveyances of spontaneous and artful creative expression. Compositionally, the two characters also pair naturally—a flourish of the **Y** serves as a crossbar within the **A**.

2 | Here, letters have been arranged so that they frame a floral illustration. Stylistic echoes between the type and image lend notes of harmony to the design.

3 | *How about combining letters from a font that already*

delivers ample conveyances of the natural world?

4 | This monogram is purely the product of font choice and arrangement. Note the subtle differences between the ornaments used in this design—differences which

understand in human terms (though to say tha

1 | Bramble   2 | Requiem   3 | Gill Floriated   4 | Papyrus, Franklin Caslon Ornaments

amplify their hand-drawn heritage (these ornaments come from a font family that contains no fewer than nine variations of this particular ornament).

5,6 | The natural world is both beautiful and harsh.

Consider leaves, thorns and all things organic when brainstorming for ways of creating a decorative border for your monogram.

7 | The building block approach used here allows for the addition of theme-boosting images and does not require the use of letters that can be structurally joined or merged.

8 | *What about creating a picture using your monogram's characters along with a few graphic add-ons?*

organic forms are ever illogical is perhaps to give

5,6 | Kuenstler Script   7 | Olduvai, Woodcut Extras   8 | custom lettering

1,2 | There are all kinds of ways of creating word graphics that are meant to deliver organic conveyances—sometimes, all you need to do is select the right font.

3 | Type can be used to do more than just spell things out. Here, letters have been employed to convey a word's essence on textual *and* visual levels. Software makes this kind of image-exploration and creation easier than ever.

4 | *What about building a pictorial scene around a phrase to emphasize its meaning?* The juxtaposition between the matter-of-fact headline and casually rendered graphic elements in this layout lend a whimsical note to the design.

Homo-Sapiens too much credit for their definition

1 | Critter 2 | Infestia 3 | Bodoni Antiqua

5 | The handwritten font used in this layout generates organic conveyances of its own. These expressions are multiplied by the text's literal meaning, its association with a nature-oriented background pattern, and a palette of natural colors. When creating word graphics, ask yourself, *how far should I take this theme? How many layers of visual expression and thematic meaning should I be aiming for?*

6 | Try out a variety of placement options when you are adding text to an image. Explore solutions that grant visual priority to the text as well as arrangements that allow the image to dominate.

f logic). In terms of visual art, organic themes

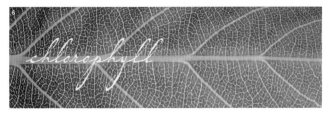

1 | The power of simplicity. *What about combining a singularly strong image with a concise textual element to create a graphic image that says enough without saying too much?*

are usually represented by contours, forms and col

5.

2 | Is there an eye-
catching way of using
the letters of your word
to build an image that
expresses the word's
meaning? Can it be done
without throwing legibility
out the window?

ors that reflect nature's adaptive and flowing ways.

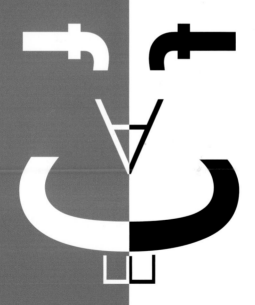

1 | The ribbon (along with the two small ornaments it contains) and the type used in this design come from different font families. The flower and stem were drawn by hand. Logos that are meant to look handcrafted are perfectly suited for improvised design conglomerations such as this.

2-4 | Some fonts carry enough thematic personality to deliver a logo's theme without the help of graphic embellishments. Explore solutions such as these—especially when a project's timeline or budget are particularly restrictive.

5 | The first letter of this company's name has been repeated, rotated and colored to create a corporate icon. Keep your eyes and

And just as life on Earth is about as varied as

1 | Caslon Antique, Olduvai Ornaments   2 | Bramble   3 | Cenizas, Franklin Gothic   4 | Sniplash

mind open for this kind of graphic opportunity when working with type. Try out different fonts to see which ones lend themselves best to the effect you are after.

6 | *How about designing your logo as a self-* contained visual environment? Consider adding images outside or inside (or both, as in this case) your logo's typographic elements.

Compositionally, the word **incorporated** has been added in a way that lends a sense of structure to the design: its height matches the stem of the **y** next to it and it has been positioned to appear centered beneath the flower (whose color it shares).

anything humanly imaginable, typefaces that

5

6

1 | If you are thinking of filling your font with theme-boosting images, consider using a typeface that is heavy enough to give the images plenty of room to show themselves. Since lighter colors were chosen for this type's interior, a

bold outline was added to help ensure proper contrast between the logotype and its backdrop.

2 | *What about fashioning your logo into a dynamic structure that's filled with a pattern of organically-*

themed embellishments? Take a look at art from cultures that have traditions of heavy ornamentation for typographic and design ideas of this sort.

3 | Organic themes need not be presented in casual

reflect organic themes are an extremely diverse

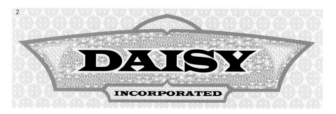

1 | Poster Paint, Myriad Tilt   2 | Wide Latin, WebOMints   3 | Requiem

visual terms. Here, a stately design has been created by framing an elegant serif typeface between a set of gracefully simplified graphic elements. The symmetrical structure of the logo projects a sense of balance

that further emphasizes its dignified ambiance.

4 | Here, the tail of the **y** has been drawn out and shaped into a relaxed floral design. One of its upper arms has also been lengthened and reshaped

so that it fills a vacant area between the two preceding letters. *How about transforming features of one or more of your logo's characters into a free-flowing swirl or shape that expresses the natural theme you are after?*

sub-species. Organically-oriented themes can

4

Organic themes can be cross-pollinated with just about any other. Here, hi-tech meets flower-power in a design that transmits conveyances that are both natural and technological. Don't fret if you're given the task of creating a logo that is supposed to deliver two or more contradictory themes—look at it as an opportunity to come up with a uniquely communicative design.

be expressed through typographic character

Bionika

hat are built from graceful, interconnected

1 | This poster's headline and subhead look as though they could be snippets of writing lifted from a journal or a personal note—their message comes across as a confidential communication between the layout and the viewer.

Hand-rendered typefaces such as these can connect with their audience on levels that might be difficult to reach using ordinary type.

2 | The hand-drawn qualities of the type and text ornaments used in

this design are subtle but powerful contributors to the design's richly organic feel.

3 | The graffiti-like typeface used here adds a counter-culture quality to the spontaneous and natural look of the layout. Note

and intuitively balanced forms. These theme

1 | Cenizas, Stanyan   2 | Olduvai, Olduvai Ornaments   3 | Ed Rogers, Franklin Caslon

that the two **o**s in the headline are different from each other—some handwritten fonts offer alternate versions of characters that can be used to add a feeling of authenticity to the (apparently) hand-lettered typeface.

4 | Even when presented in all caps, the gracefully crafted forms of this headline's characters deliver pleasantly natural conveyances. Inferences of modernity are expressed by the lack of word-spacing and the color-shifts within the text, while a hint of tradition is imparted by the aged ornaments above the header.

5 | *What about an approach that tightly integrates your design's type and image?*

an also be delivered through fonts that feature

4 | Goudy, Franklin Caslon Ornaments   5 | Olduvai

Organic themes connect well to compositional strategies that reflect nature's adaptive and spontaneous ways. In this design, the headline has been written by hand, and, instead of flowing from left to right, it follows the model's gaze. Aligned with this rule-breaking header is a subhead whose rightward-leaning italic characters counteract the leftward movement of the headline. Explore typographic solutions that are both obedient to the rules of design and those that eschew order in favor of inventive and offbeat expressions.

literal visual expressions related to plants, animals

Century Schoolbook, hand-lettered type

nsects and human beings within their forms.

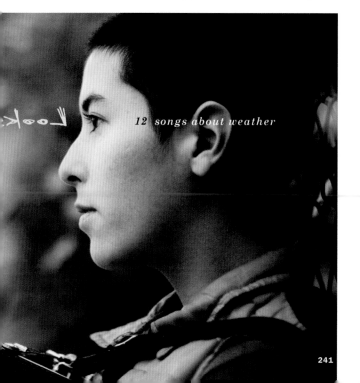

12 songs about weather

1-4 | There's a progression among the four announcements in this set that demonstrates how varying levels of organic-ness can be channeled into a design via different typographic and design approaches. The set begins with a good-natured layout built using a traditional font family that includes both openface and standard typefaces [1]. The next design appears a tad more home-spun with its stitched-looking border (assembled from text ornaments) and the addition of a few nature-oriented decorations [2]. Folksy conveyances are further amplified In the third sample where the subtext's font has been changed to a hand-lettered typeface and a loosely rendered ornament has been inserted

There are also a number of fonts whose desig

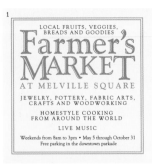

1 | Goudy   2 | Goudy, Hoefler Ornaments   3 | Goudy, Bramble, Franklin Caslon Ornaments

into the layout's backdrop [3]. The organic look-and-feel of the final design is raised to yet another level by releasing most of the layout's elements from the strictures of any sort of compositional grid [4].

5 | Digitally-generated type can be made to look hand-rendered using (ironically enough) digital effects. This layout's headline has been roughed-up in Photoshop to give it a look reminiscent of old-style letterpress or woodblock printing. A font that likewise appears to have been rendered by hand is used for the sub-text. These elements, along with the loosely-drawn carrot in the background, amount to a clearly non-corporate announcement for a neighborhood market.

could best be described as non-mechanical or

5

FARMER'S

Local fruits, veggies, breads and goodies * Jewelry, Pottery, Woodworking, Fabrics and Crafts of all kinds * Homestyle cooking from around the world * Live music * Weekends from 8am to 3pm * May 5 through October 31 * Free parking in the downtown parkade

MARKET

at Melville Square

1 | Down-to-earth people tend to connect with the grassroots conveyances of designs that appear to have been created by hand. If this demographic is your target audience, consider creating a layout that is (or appears to be) entirely handcrafted. Only the extremely observant—and those familiar with font design—are likely to realize that no pencil, pen or brush were involved in the creation of this computer-generated composition.

non-computer-generated that could also be considered

1

FARMER'S MARKET

LOCAL FRUITS, VEGGIES,
BREADS AND GOODIES

JEWELRY, POTTERY, FABRIC ARTS,
CRAFTS AND WOODWORKING

HOMESTYLE COOKING
FROM AROUND THE WORLD

LIVE MUSIC

MELVILLE SQUARE

Weekends from 8am to 3pm • May 5 through October 31
Free parking in the downtown parkade

2 | How about creating a graphic element that provides a funky visual framework for your text while acting as a theme-setter for its message? The fonts used in this layout were selected based on their visual and conceptual connection with the style of illustration used in the design.

organically-inclined. Another typographic category

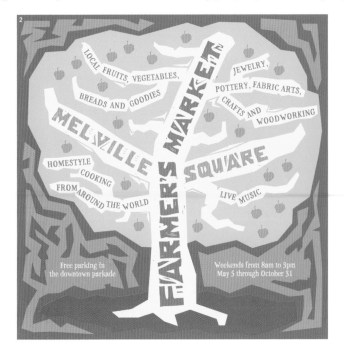

The conversational tone of this text* seems well suited to a presentation through fonts whose origins lie in handwritten letterforms.

The hand-printed, felt-tip style of this font comes across as informal and spontaneous [1]. The next two samples express themselves in more refined terms and look as though they were penned by a trained and artistic hand [2,3]. The arsty conveyances of some handwritten type- faces are amplified through visual suggestions that the text was rendered with a calligraphic tool of some sort (note the varying weights among the forms of these letters) [4].

that conveys plenty of nature-based connotation

1

The daily menu is posted on large blackboards, as the entrées change with every meal. There are always at least two soups, and both fresh fruit and vegetable salad bowls (meals in themselves), as well as three to four (sometimes more) entrées. Freshly baked, whole-grain bread (made down the hall, at Somadhara Bakery) is always on hand. Beer and wine, as well as bottled water and fruit juices, are

2

served. Some desserts are sweetened with sugar, others, with honey or real maple syrup. (Moosewood is the only place in town where you can follow up an herbed soybean casserole with a rich, dense, authentically-chocolate fudge brownie.) Every Sunday evening is "ethnic night," with an entire menu—desserts included—devoted exclusively to the cuisine of one country or ethnic group.

---

*Excerpted from the foreword of one of the most popular vegetarian cookbooks of all time, **Moosewood Cookbook**, by Mollie Katzen.

1 | Felt Tip   2 | Luce

Typefaces based on hand-writing come in a vast range of styles and each projects a unique visual voice. If you are looking for just the right handwritten font for a particular piece of text, and are having a hard time selecting one based on a mere showing of a font's alphabet, you might want to shop at a website that allows you to try out a typeface (on-screen) before purchasing it. Many online font stores provide interactive try-before-you-buy font testing portals.

is that of text ornaments. In fact, it's a rare family

3

The daily menu is posted on large blackboards, as the entrées change with every meal. There are always at least two soups, and both fresh fruit and vegetable salad bowls (meals in themselves), as well as three to four (sometimes more) entrées. Freshly baked, whole-grain bread (made down the hall, at Domadhara

4

Bakery) is always on hand. Beer and wine, as well as bottled water and fruit juices, are served. Some desserts are sweetened with sugar, others, with honey or real maple syrup. (Moosewood is the only place in town where you can follow up an herbed soybean casserole with a rich, dense, authentically-chocolate fudge brownie.) Every Sunday evening is "ethnic night," with an entire menu—desserts included—devoted exclusively to the cuisine of one country or ethnic group.

1 | Some handcrafted typefaces look as though they were created by a truly free-spirited hand. These typefaces often seem far less concerned with proper penmanship than with personal expression. Both the type and the leaf featured in this design come from the same highly original font family.

The quantity of informal, improvised, hand-lettered fonts available on the typographic scene seems to be expanding by leaps and bounds (perhaps in reaction to the ever-increasing and exacting influence of computers). If fonts such as these interest you, keep tabs on the latest offerings of foundries that specialize in this kind of anti-technology design.

of text ornaments whose images and decoration.

1

THE **DAILY MENU** IS POSTED ON LARGE BLACKBOARDS, AS THE ENTRÉES CHANGE WITH EVERY MEAL. THERE ARE ALWAYS AT LEAST TWO **SOUPS**, AND BOTH **FRESH FRUIT** AND **VEGETABLE SALAD** BOWLS (MEALS IN THEMSELVES), AS WELL AS THREE TO FOUR (SOMETIMES MORE) ENTRÉES. FRESHLY BAKED, **WHOLE-GRAIN BREAD** (MADE DOWN THE HALL, AT SOMADHARA BAKERY) IS ALWAYS ON HAND. **BEER AND WINE**, AS WELL AS BOTTLED WATER AND FRUIT JUICES, ARE SERVED. SOME **DESSERTS** ARE SWEETENED WITH SUGAR, OTHERS, WITH HONEY OR REAL MAPLE SYRUP. (MOOSEWOOD IS THE ONLY PLACE IN TOWN WHERE YOU CAN FOLLOW UP AN HERBED SOYBEAN CASSEROLE WITH A RICH, DENSE, AUTHENTICALLY-CHOCOLATE FUDGE BROWNIE.) EVERY SUNDAY EVENING IS "**ETHNIC NIGHT**," WITH AN ENTIRE MENU—— DESSERTS INCLUDED——DEVOTED EXCLUSIVELY TO THE CUISINE OF ONE COUNTRY OR ETHNIC GROUP.

2 | Typefaces that have little or no connection with a hand-rendered or organic heritage can also be presented in ways that deliver natural connotations—sometimes it's just a matter of applying the right palette of earthy colors to your non-organic typeface.

3 | *Could your typeface use more of an organic boost than those provided by an earthy palette alone?* If so, consider adorning your paragraph with an initial cap or background elements (or both, as in this case) that add further natural connotations to your design.

do not include a healthy measure of horticulture-

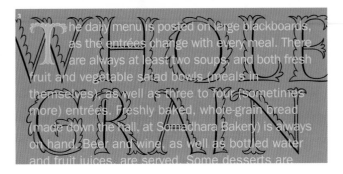

2 The daily menu is posted on large blackboards, as the entrées change with every meal. There are always at least two soups, and both fresh fruit and vegetable salad bowls (meals in themselves), as well as three to four (sometimes more) entrées. Freshly baked, whole-grain bread (made down the hall, at Somadhara Bakery) is always on hand. Beer and wine, as well as bottled water and fruit juices, are served. Some desserts are sweetened with sugar, others with

3 The daily menu is posted on large blackboards, as the entrées change with every meal. There are always at least two soups, and both fresh fruit and vegetable salad bowls (meals in themselves), as well as three to four (sometimes more) entrées. Freshly baked, whole-grain bread (made down the hall, at Somadhara Bakery) is always on hand. Beer and wine, as well as bottled water and fruit juices, are served. Some desserts are

1 | Elegance meets earthiness in this design. A refined script delivers the layout's textual message while a chalky portrait of a plump pear serves as a theme-setting masthead for the composition.

Given the text's close spatial association with the natural-looking image in this layout, other fonts could have been used without threatening the organic conveyances of this presentation. Tasty serif typefaces (italic or roman),

thin sans serif fonts or informal handwritten faces would all be worthy of consideration.

based heritage in its bloodline. Nature's influence o

1

The daily menu is posted on large blackboards, as the entrées change with every meal. There are always at least two soups, and both fresh fruit and vegetable salad bowls (meals in themselves), as well as three to four (sometimes more) entrées. Freshly baked, whole-grain bread (made down the hall, at Somadhara Bakery) is always on hand. Beer and wine, as well as bottled water and fruit juices, are served. Some desserts are sweetened with sugar, others, with honey or real maple syrup. (Moosewood is the only place in town where you can follow up an herbed soybean casserole with a rich, dense, authentically-chocolate fudge brownie.) Every Sunday evening is "ethnic night," with an entire menu – desserts included – devoted exclusively to the cuisine of one country or ethnic group.

1 | Edwardian Script

2 | Type and illustration become one in this layout. A hand-rendered serif font has been chosen to complement the spontaneous quality of illustration. The type has been given a slightly bulging quality (using Photoshop's SPHERIZE filter) to highlight its connection to the pear's form. Photoshop was also used to create a dark halo around the type (using the OUTER GLOW command) to help it stand out against the visually active surface of the pear.

he design of letters and images has been resonating

Infuse your organic page designs with attributes of the natural world.

1,2 | Nature is informal. Consider creating a casual environment for your formal typefaces. Loosen things up even more by further relaxing the composition's structure and switching to a funky headline font.

3 | Nature (often) means open spaces. Space permitting, set aside generous portions of your design for large, theme setting images and/or patterns. (The pattern featured here is built from birds borrowed from an image-oriented font family.)

4 | *Nature means no boundaries. How about letting a graphic element encroach on your type's territory?*

with viewers since the days of the illuminated manuscript (and before), and continues to do so through the printed and electronic media of today. And why not? Our very perception of visual grace and aesthetic harmor

1

2

This compact, colorful and graceful flyer is also a fish's worst nightmare.

the
Belted Kingfisher

Abc def ghijk lm nop qr stuv wxy zabc defgh ij klmno pqrst uv w xy zab cd efg h ijk lm no pqr st uvw xy zabcd ef gh ijk lm nop qr st uv wxy zabc d ef gh ij klmno pqrst uv w xy zab cd efghijk lm n op qrs.

Abc def ghijk lm nop qr stuv wxy zabc defgh ij klmno pqrst uv w xy zab cd efg h ijk lm no pqr st uvw xy zabcd ef gh ijk lm nop qr st uv wxy zabc d ef gh ij klmno pqrst uv w xy zab cd efghijk lm n op q r st uvw xy zabcd ef ghijk lm nop qr stuv wxy zabc defgh ij klmno pqrst uv

xy zab cd efg h ijk lm no pqr st uvw xy zabcd ef gh ijk lm nop qr st uv wxy zabc d ef gh ij klmno pqrst uv w xy zab cd efghijk lm n op q r st uvw xy zabcd ef ghijk lm nop qr stuv wxy zabc defgh ij klmno pqrst uv w xy zab cd efg h ijk lm no pqr st uvw xy zabcd ef gh ijk lm nop qr st uv wxy zab cd efg h ijk lm n op qr st

wxy zabc d ef gh ijk lmnop qrst uv w xy zab cd efghijk lm n op q r st uvw xy zabcd ef ghijk lm nop qr stuv wxy zabc de fgh ij klm no pq rst lm nopqr st uvw xy zabcd ef ghijk lm nop qr stuv wxy zabc def ghijk lm nop qr stuv wxy zabc defgh ij klmno pqrst uv w xy zab cd efg h ijk lm no pqr st uv wxy zabc d ef gh ij klmno pqrst uv w xy zab cd efghijk lm n op q r st

Abc def ghijk lm nop qr stuv wxy zabc defgh ij klmno pqrst uv w xy zab cd efg h ijk lm no pqr st uvw xy zabcd ef gh ijk lm no pqr st uvw xy zabcd ef ghijk lm nop qr stuv wxy zabc defgh ij klmno pqrst uv

---

rises from cues given to us by the natural world.

the
BELTED
KINGFISHER

This compact, colorful and graceful flyer is also a fish's worst nightmare.

Abc def ghijk lm nop qr stuv wxy zabc defgh ij klmno pqrst uv w xy zab cd efg h ijk lm no pqr st uvw xy zabcd ef gh ijk lm nop qr st uv wxy zabc d ef gh ij klmno pqrst uv w xy zab cd efghijk lm n op q r st uvw xy zabcd ef ghijk lm nop qr stuv wxy zabc defgh ij klmno pqrst uv

st uvw xy zabcd ef gh ijk lm nop qr st uv wxy zabc d ef gh ij klmno pqrst uv w xy zab cd efghijk lm n op q r st uvw xy zabcd ef ghijk lm nop qr stuv wxy zabc defgh ij klmno pqrst uv w xy zab cd efg h ijk lm no pqr st uvw xy zabcd ef ghijk lm

lm nop qr st uv wxy zabc d ef gh ij klmno pqrst uv w xy zab cd efghijk lm n op q r st uvw xy zabcd ef ghijk lm nop qr stuv wxy zabc defgh ij klmno pqrst uv w xy zab cd efg h ijk lm no pqr st uvw xy zabcd ef ghijk lm nop qr st uv wxy zabc d ef gh ij klmno pqrst uv w xy zab cd efghijk lm n op q r st uvw xy zabcd ef ghijk lm nopqr st uvw xy zabc def ghijk lm nop qr stuv wxy zabc defgh ij klmno pqrst uv w xy zab cd efg

h ijk lm no pqr st uvw xy zabcd ef gh ijk lm nop qr st uv wxy zabc d ef gh ij klmno pqrst uv w xy zab cd efghijk lm n op q r st uvw xy zabcd ef ghijk lm nop qr stuv wxy zabc defgh ij klmno pqrst uv w xy zab cd efghijk lm nop qr stuv wxy zabc defgh ij klmno pqrst uv w xy zab cd efg h ijk lm no pqr st uvw xy zabcd ef gh ij klmno pqrst uv w xy zab cd efghijk lm.

Abc def ghijk lm nop qr stuv wxy zab cd efgh ij klmno pqr st uvw xy zabcd ef gh ijk.

Fonts used in this chapter:

One representative is shown for each typeface family.

SERIF TYPEFACES

Bodoni Antiqua

Caslon Antique

Century Schoolbook

Cochin

ENGRAVERS MT

Goudy

Hoefler

Requiem

Wide Latin

SANS SERIF

Franklin Gothic

Frutiger

Futura

Gill Sans

Helvetica

Impact

Knockout

SCRIPT, HANDLETTERED AND CALLIGRAPHIC

Bramble

Cenizas

Dearest

ED ROGERS

Edwardian Script

Felt Tip

Freestyle Script

Kuenstler Script

Klang

Luce

Lucida Handwriting

Ministry Script

Mr. Leopolde

Mr. Sheppards

NOVELTY, DISPLAY

Bionika

CRITTER

Franklin Caslon

Infestia

Kamaro

Myriad Tilt

Olduvai

Papyrus

POSTER PAINT

Sniplash

Stanyan

WOODCUT SANS

ORNAMENT FONTS
Ballywick
Cloister Initials
Constructivist Extras
Delectables
Ed Rogers Ornaments
Franklin Caslon Ornaments
Gill Floriated Capitals
Hoefler Ornaments
Insectile
Olduvai Ornaments
WebOMints
Woodcut Extras

FOCUS ON:
Core Essentials

Extended font families* can be both extraordinarily useful and prohibitively expensive. The good news for designers (particularly those who pay for their own typefaces) is that an effective font library can be built by establishing a core collection of just two to four of these versatile sets and augmenting them with a variety of less costly typefaces that serve specialized purposes.

At the backbone of many designer's personal font cache are at least a few extended serif font families. Font sets of this kind can provide typefaces for everything from bold headlines to slender italic subheads to highly legible body text. If you already have one such font family and want to add another to your type library, look for a font set that is decidedly different—but equally as functional—as the one(s) you already own. The two topmost fonts highlighted on the following page provide a good example of just such a complementary pair of serif type families. A duo such as this could be used to serve a truly broad range of compositional and communicative roles.

One or two versatile and varied extended sans serif families are also considered must-have components in the type collection of many design pros. Characters from one such collection are featured on the following spread.

Designers with a more-or-less typical client roster often find that the most effective typefaces to have at the core of their collection are those whose style leans toward the traditional and project a relatively neutral visual personality. Fonts such as these usually have a longer shelf life than newfangled designs and tend to perform well in supporting roles when paired with more expressive and attention-demanding fonts. Ideally, the fonts in a designer's core

*Extended font families often include a dozen or more variations of a particular typeface (see the samples on the next page). These variations usually include a font's full range of weights and italic (or oblique) versions of each weight. These sets might also include condensed versions of a font as well as an assortment of text ornaments that echo the font's design.

collection will be capable of serving a wide range of compositional and thematic needs. Still, nearly all designers need to expand their library beyond a core of essential fonts to include typefaces that can be used to cover the full creative spectrum of their work. These special-purpose fonts come in handy for everything from logo design to the creation of expressive headlines; from custom word graphics to eye-catching text presentations.

A designer's font library is most effective when it is populated—from the core outward—with fonts that reflect that artist's creative style while also providing an adequate range of expression to meet the needs of their client-based work.

Hoefler Text

Aa *Aa Aa*
Roman, roman italic,
roman swash

Aa *Aa Aa*
Roman small caps, italic
small caps, swash small caps

Aa *Aa Aa*
Bold, bold italic,
bold swash

Aa *Aa Aa*
Bold small caps, bold italic small
caps, bold swash small caps

Aa *Aa Aa*
Black, black italic,
black swash

Aa *Aa Aa*
Black small caps, black italic small
caps, black swash small caps

A A
Engraved,
Engraved two

Ornaments and fleurons

Bodoni

Aa *Aa*
Light,
light italic

Aa *Aa*
Regular,
regular italic

Aa *Aa*
Medium and
medium italic

Aa
Bold

Aa
Extra
Bold

Aa
Ultra
Bold

Aa
Poster
compressed

Franklin Gothic

Aa Aa
Book,
book italic

Aa Aa
Medium,
medium italic

Aa Aa
Demi,
demi italic

Aa Aa
Heavy,
Heavy italic

Aa Aa
Book condensed,
book cond. italic

Aa Aa
Medium condensed,
medium cond. italic

Aa Aa
Demi condensed,
demi cond. italic

Aa Aa
Book compressed,
book comp. italic

Aa Aa
Demi compressed,
demi comp. italic

Aa Aa
Book extra-compressed,
Demi extra-compressed

CHAPTER 7

Specific Eras

Projecting themes related to **specific eras, social and art movements** and **kitsch** through type and its supporting compositional elements.

1 | The design of this character is based on letterforms that were drawn centuries before the first hand-carved typefaces were used on Gutenberg's press. For the most part, connotations of history are unquestioningly accepted by viewers who could care less whether a calligraphic-looking typeface was created with a quill, chisel, drafting pen or computer.

2-4 | The thick and thin strokes of serif typefaces are direct descendents of the calligraphic and carved letterforms of earlier eras. To modern eyes, certain serif faces appear more old-world than others—conveyances of tradition and history can be projected through pronounced serifs and

Relative to world history, typefaces haven't bee

1 | Duc De Berry   2 | Charlemagne   3 | Caslon Antique   4 | Castellar

organic curves [2], a weathered, aged appearance [3], and connotations of a chiseled origin [4].

5-9 | Memorable eras are often connected to typefaces that grew from the artistic and cultural temperament of those times. When working on a project that calls for conveyances associated with a particular era, consider amplifying expressions of that time period through typefaces that embody its spirit.

10 | Some eras have yet to occur. Futuristic themes can transmitted by typefaces that fit our current perception of how letterforms might be affected the trends of tomorrow.

around for all that long. It wasn't until Gutenberg

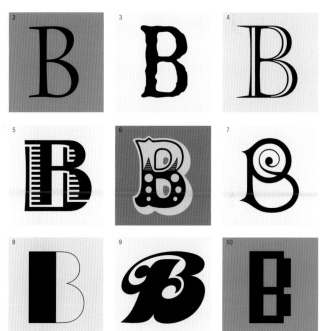

1 | Here, an archival character has been used as a corporate icon. This old-world letter lends notes of a credible heritage to the logo—a theme complemented by the modern (though still traditional) typeface used for the company's name.

2 | The old-style typeface that was used for the previous logo's icon has been used to spell out the company's name in this sample. The icon in this design is built from a modern character. Combinations of age-old and modern-age typefaces can generate era-spanning artistic and thematic conveyances.

SEE COMBINING FONTS, PAGE 212.

3 | *Trying to project the ambiance of a certain time period through a logo? Consider constructing your*

invented the printing press in the early 1600s tha

1

2

3

4

5

1 | Fette Fraktur, Requiem, Requiem Ornaments   2 | Fette Fraktur, Aviner   3 | Kismet   4,5 | Futura

design—icon and all—using a single typeface that embodies the spirit of that era.

4,5 | Conveyances from the dawn of the scientific age can be expressed through pseudo-technical effects such as basic 3D structures and cast shadows. Consider applying effects such as these to individual letters, logos or headlines.

6 | The letter **m** from this futuristic font makes a dramatic and intriguing icon for a casually modernistic logo. The typeface used in this design was created in the 1960s. A half-century later it still projects a progressive sense of modernity—though not without an acquired hint of kitsch.

the need for standardized sets of reusable letters

6

History has seen the creation of countless intriguing letter designs that do not belong to any particular font family. These characters can be especially useful as theme-setting initial caps or as decorative background elements for layouts. Look to printed and online sources for non-copyrighted characters such as these.

came into being. Since those times, the science and

All samples: custom letters

art of typography have been in a state of constant

1 | Historically-inspired fonts make natural choices for monograms—multi-letter designs have been around since the earliest days of lettering and typography.

2 | This composition projects implications of a rich historical lineage through its age-old form of graphic expression. Just as particular fonts are associated with specific time periods, so too are certain kinds of graphic structures.

3 | Time-proven design motifs tend to have broad appeal. An old-world design such as this might be equally at home as a label for a modern music promoter as it would be as a logo for a century-old tableware manufacturer.

growth and change—an evolutionary process that

4 | Every so often, designers are asked to create a logo for a company whose initials lend themselves effortlessly to an intriguing compositional arrangement. To capitalize on the design-opportunity presented by this company's initials, a perfectly symmetrical monogram was created by stacking an upside-down **W** over an **M**.

5 | *How about employing multiple fonts from a single era when creating a monogram that aims to reflect* the mood of a specific time period?

6,7 | *What about mixing the old and the new?* Consider filling—or adorning—contemporary letterforms with ornate decorations from the past.

has always been linked to the prevailing technical

Mademoiselle
Wearables

Explore various typographic options when you are trying to decide how to accompany initials with the words they stand for.

1 | *How about spelling out your company's name with the same font that was used for its monogram?* Using a single font amplifies the thematic and stylistic projections coming from a design's typography. Sometimes this is a good thing; sometimes it's too much of a good thing.

2 | The personality of this logo has been broadened by using different fonts for the monogram and company's name. The fonts pair well since they are visually different but thematically linked (both exude conveyances of civility and tradition).

know-how and artistic/cultural temperament o

Duc De Berry (used in all monograms on next page)

3 | Here again, two different fonts—both of which agree on traditional conveyances of elegance—are used within one logo design. The delicate linework and dramatic black panel that frame this composition's type generate further expressions of refinement.

4 | The structure of this logo allows for a congenial separation between the two radically different—and potentially conflicting—styles of type used in the composition. Numerous agreeable connotations arise from this pairing of a progressive and archival font: forward thinking modernity; archival credibility and quality; and artistic flair.

he times. Today, typefaces whose forms evoke the

1

2

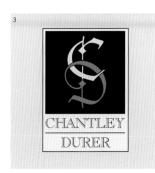

3

4

1 | Fonts from a specific era often reflect cultural styles and moods that were prevalent during that time. When creating word graphics, consider using a typeface whose era-based visual personality enforces the tone and meaning

your text is meant to express.

2 | The message of this invented word is amplified through a font that places it in a specific cultural and time-sensitive context. Try out fonts that speak your

word graphic's message in a voice and style that echoes its era-evoking message. Fonts related to certain time periods can be employed to add humorous, sarcastic, playful, novel or kitschy overtones to text.

ambiance of bygone eras (regardless of whethe

1 | Manhattan   2 | Motter Femina   3 | Fette Fraktur

3 | Contemporary ads, bumper stickers and T-shirts are often used as venues for lighthearted era-mixing. Here, a modern day phrase gains regal notes of finality when set in an old-world typeface.

4-9 | The personality of some words can be greatly influenced though fonts that place them in the context of different time periods. Experiment, and explore! Seek ideas and inspiration by looking at examples of typography and design from the era you are trying to invoke.

hose fonts were designed yesteryear or yesterday)

Is there a cultural movement from the past whose graphic trends can be tapped into to enhance the meaning and visual presentation of your word(s) (whether for the purposes of historical accuracy or kitsch)? This graphic was built entirely of letters and ornaments from a type family inspired by the art of early Soviet era graphic artists.

can be called upon to convey moods and expression.

Constructivist, Constructivist Extras

from past times. You don't have to look far to see

OLT

1-6 | What might each of these logos be saying about the kind of dance taught at this studio? The purpose of this spread is simple: to demonstrate the effect that era-specific fonts can have on a logo's conveyances of meaning and context.

When creating a logo, ask yourself, *could this company be effectively represented through a font from a specific era? If so, where can I find a selection of fonts from this time period to choose from?* (As you might expect, the web is an excellent place to start your search for archival typefaces.)

examples of era-based fonts being used in design and

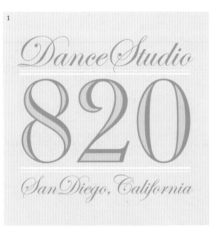

1 | Edwardian Script, Castellar   2 | Rennie Mackintosh   3 | Arnold Boecklin, Desdemona   4 | Jazz

advertising for just such purposes. Typefaces can

1,2 | When designing for a company with a heritage rooted in old-world traditions of craftsmanship and quality, consider using typefaces whose characters are likewise built according to time-proven standards.

To create the treble clef used as an icon in this design, modifications were made to a capital **S** (from the same font as was used for the logo [**2**]. A detail borrowed from an **L** provided this symbol with its finishing flourish. The

result is an icon that melds nicely with the logo's type.

3-6 | What if Trillium was a company that produced a variety of stringed instruments—models ranging in design from traditional to cutting-edge? And what if

also be summoned to stir up recollections o

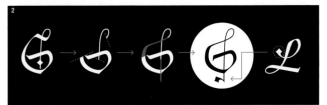

1,2 | Duc De Berry

this company was looking for a cohesive and descriptive set of logos to represent their century-spanning product line? Era-based fonts could be just the thing needed to solve a design challenge such as this.

A corporate version of the logo [3] has been built using an artful (though not era-specific) typeface. Time-period-sensitive versions of this logo were then created by adding era-invoking type to a panel that has been

tucked in between the company's name and the logo's subtext. Additional thematic boost could be added to any of these designs through graphic additions, such as the background in the final sample.

eras that are older than typography itself.

1 | Consider using archival typefaces, ornaments and illustrations to connect a company's name with its rich historical heritage (whether that heritage is real or imagined). Here, a lavish setting has been created for two elegant typefaces by framing them with an ornate 19th century border.

2 | *How about using an archival image as the centerpiece of your logo?* The font that circles this illustration projects dual conveyances: modernity (through its contemporary sans serif structure), and tradition (through its faux-chiseled, openface design). A script font has been inserted into the layout to add notes of variety and elegance to the composition.

Many typefaces reflect hand-drawn, calligraphi

1 | Requiem, Edwardian Script   2 | Industria, Bodoni Antiqua, Edwardian Script   3 | Patriot, Edwardian Script

3 | This logo features age-old ideas that have been given a modern spin: Its primary typeface contains a number of details borrowed from archival fonts (note the old-world lowercase **t**s and the subtle extensions to the **L**s, **E**s and **F**); the historically-inspired wreath of laurels that circles the type has been illustrated in a contemporary style; and finally, a modern—though still traditional—script initial has been added to convey a touch of flourish.

4 | Decorative scrolls can be used to separate textual elements, frame a design and establish a theme of traditional elegance.

and stone-carved letterforms that predate the

4

1,2 | This pair of straight-forward poster layouts is intended to prompt the sort of questions designers might ask themselves when considering ways of conveying nostalgia through typography. Questions such as, *How much nostalgia is enough? How much nostalgia is too much? Where is the line between nostalgia and corniness? Should all of the fonts in the design look like yesteryear's typefaces? Should "era-neutral" typefaces be combined with old world fonts and/or images? Would a mix of progressive and traditional typefaces generate a look that complements the design's message? What about decorative elements and color choices—should these be old-style, contemporary or timeless?*

invention of mass-produced letterforms by centuries.

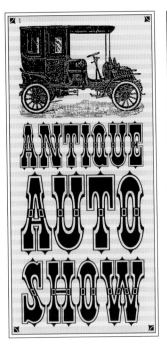

1 | Pepperwood   2 | Knockout

3-6 | Weigh your conceptual options when you design around a particular time period. Consider solutions that involve fonts, images and colors that look as though they have sprung from the same era [3]. Think about combining a contemporary font with an aged-looking image to generate an offbeat or counterculture feel [4]. *What about reaching for a futuristic look by applying digital effects to your image and pairing it with a cyber-era typeface [5]?* Explore ideas that involve graphic elements, images and type from unrelated time periods (after all, who says that a design has to be perfectly logical in order to be eye-catching and communicative [6]?

There are many typefaces that project conveyances

3 | Motter Femina   4 | Ed Rogers   5 | Bionika   6 | Duc De Berry

that are both historic and modern. Typefaces such

Designers aren't the only ones who occasionally take typography from one era and place it in a setting from another. Sometimes nature and time do it on their own.

as these are often built by detailing contemporary

1,2 | There is hardly an era that cannot be visually expressed—in an assortment of thematic flavors—through typography. Compare these two poster designs. The first features type that is true to the time period it represents; the second makes use of a contemporary font/image collection that applies a kitschy twist to the design's wild-west conveyances. Explore options when you are selecting era-based type for your design: Consider fonts that are authentic representatives of your time period, as well as typefaces that add a silly, humorous or sarcastic thematic spin.

3 | Long before the era of the printing press and

letterforms with ornaments, extensions or fills that

1 | Pepperwood, BlackOak, Rosewood   2 | Way Out West, Way Out West Critters

moveable type, announcements and proclamations were inked with natural brushes or carved with metal tools. The look of the typeface used in this design is based on chiseled letterforms that pre-date the Gutenberg press

by several centuries. This font makes an appropriate choice for a poster that promotes a series of events dealing with the pre-printing press days of Western literature.

4 | *How about sending the look of your design back in time by giving it a faux dimensional/textural makeover in Photoshop? (A little digital wizardry can go a long way—be careful not to overdo it!)*

are reminiscent of archival alphabets. Given the

1 | The heritage of this design's primary font is rooted in the social scene of 1900s Paris—its extroverted visual personality still radiates conveyances of art house chic. The addition of a subtle (and relevant) image to the poster's background serves compositional and conceptual purposes as it forms a visual connector between the headline and supporting text while enforcing the geographic context of the design.

2 | Art nouveau, through and through. Colors, typefaces and border elements work in unison to confirm the era-based theme of this layout.

A relatively modern font has been used for the words **Literary Club** and all

vast quantity of era-based fonts in existence, and

1 | Kismet, Benguiat Gothic   2 | Kismet, Arnold Boecklin, Benguiat Gothic

of the supporting text in this design. This font (Benguiat Gothic) was created in the 1970s and its forms are based on those found in typefaces that arose during the heyday of art nouveau. More legible than many true nouveau fonts, this typeface works nicely as a deliverer of important textual information in the context of this nostalgia-evoking design.

3,4 | Consider solutions that leave ample breathing room around your era-based typography—as well as those that pack your design's environs with type. *Is one approach more in keeping with the artistic norms of the era you are designing toward—or are you working with a time period that grants leeway in terms of compositional choices?*

the huge range of expression that can be delivered

1 | Only time will tell which typefaces are going to stick around after the initial fanfare of their introduction has faded. Time seems to have spoken on behalf of the innovative typographic and design styles that grew out of the social/political/artistic environment of early twentieth-century Eastern Europe. Designers regularly draw upon fonts and design conventions from this era when visual expressions of activism and revolution are being sought.

through those fonts, this chapter can only scratch

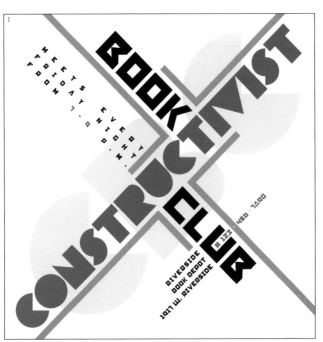

1 | Constructivist

2 | Future eras seem to grant the most freedom in terms of typographic, compositional and conceptual parameters (after all, tradition hasn't had a chance to develop in times that have yet to occur).

Futuristic and archival fonts have been combined—one directly on top of the other—in this forward-thinking design. This typographic/compositional approach seems fitting given that it is being used to

promote a series of cyber-themed literary events that take place in a setting derived from the time of King Arthur.

the surface of the topic of era-based type and design.

2 | Python, Fette Fraktur, Joystick

What better sample of text to use in this era-spanning chapter than a two-thousand-year-old commentary on the human condition*— one that sounds as though it were written just yesterday?

Certain time periods are associated with specific human qualities: wisdom, spirituality, creativity, inventiveness, aggression, whimsy. Era-based fonts can be used to infuse textual messages with conveyances such as these.

1 | This text was originally transcribed with brush and ink—centuries before hand-carved typefaces were used on the first hand-cranked printing presses. A pseudo brush-and-ink typeface is a reasonable selection for bringing

If you feel drawn to the typography of a specific

1

I cannot tell if what the world considers "happiness" is happiness or not. All I know is that when I consider the way they go about attaining it, I see them carried away headlong, grim and obsessed, in the general onrush of the human herd, unable to stop themselves or to change their direction. All the while they claim to be just on the point of attaining happiness.

My opinion is that you never find happiness until you stop looking for it. My greatest happiness consists precisely in doing nothing whatever that is calculated to obtain happiness: and this, in the mind of most people, is the worst possible course.

*The text featured in this section is from **The Way of Chuang Tzu**, by Thomas Merton.

1 | Papyrus

its message to readers of today—complete with inferences—its ancient heritage.

2 | Old-world fonts often contain different (though recognizable) versions of some of today's alphabetic characters. Certain modern fonts channel these ancient conveyances by featuring some of these letter design relics. When using a faux (or authentic) archival typeface, be wary of legibility issues: while these fonts might be permitted to challenge readability, they should never defeat it.

3 | Calligraphic fonts are obvious choices to consider when you want to infuse text with age-old conveyances of authenticity, authority or wisdom.

time period, or have an interest in learning more

2

I CANN⊕+ +ELL IF WHA+
"HAPPINESS" IS HAPPINES:
IS +HA+ WHEN I C⊕NSIDE
AB⊕U+ A++AINING I+, I
HEADL⊕NG, GRIM AND ⊕B
⊕NRUSH ⊕F +HE HUᎷAN
+HEᎷSELVES ⊕R +⊕ CHAᎷ
+HE WHILE +HEY CLAIᎷ
⊕F A++AINING HAPPINE
ᎷY ⊕PINI⊕N IS +HA+
HAPPINESS UN+IL Y⊕U S+
GREA+ES+ HAPPINESS C⊕
N⊕+HING WHA+EVER +H/
HAPPINESS: AND +HIS, IN
Ꮇ⊕S+ PE⊕PLE, IS +HE W⊕

3

the world considers s or not. All I know is r the way they go about see them carried away essed, in the general herd, unable to stop ge their direction. All to be just on the point ss.

you never find op looking for it. My nsists precisely in doing at is calculated to obtain the mind of rst possible course.

1 | Consider building a graphic environment to complement and frame your era-based text. Note: The art nouveau typeface used for this textual sample is a display font (one designed primarily for headlines and short bits of featured text). Generally, it's considered typographically out-of-bounds to use a display font for text. Still, if a certain display typeface seems legible as a text font, and it projects conveyances that are true to your design's theme… then why not give it a try?

2 | *Instead of using an overtly era-transmitting typeface for your text, how about employing an initial cap to set the time period for your words? This*

about the history of letters and type, look to

1

I CANNOT TELL IF WHAT THE WORLD CONSIDERS "HAPPINESS"
IS HAPPINESS OR NOT. ALL I KNOW IS THAT WHEN I CONSIDER
THE WAY THEY GO ABOUT ATTAINING IT, I SEE THEM CARRIED
AWAY HEADLONG, GRIM AND OBSESSED, IN THE GENERAL
ONRUSH OF THE HUMAN HERD, UNABLE TO STOP THEMSELVES
OR TO CHANGE THEIR DIRECTION. ALL THE WHILE THEY CLAIM
TO BE JUST ON THE POINT OF ATTAINING HAPPINESS.
MY OPINION IS THAT YOU NEVER FIND HAPPINESS UNTIL
YOU STOP LOOKING FOR IT. MY GREATEST HAPPINESS
CONSISTS PRECISELY IN DOING NOTHING WHATEVER THAT IS
CALCULATED TO OBTAIN HAPPINESS: AND THIS, IN THE MIND
OF MOST PEOPLE, IS THE WORST POSSIBLE COURSE.

1 | Rennie Mackintosh

particular capital does not belong to any font family, but rather was scanned from a book of permission-free archival type samples.

3 | The sample text used in this section projects a whole new feel when it is set in a futuristic typeface. Here, the text seems more like commentary from a perceptive source of artificial intelligence than the words of a third-century (B.C.) Chinese philosopher.

Take a look at what happens when your age-old message is featured in a font from a radically different era—do intriguing or amusing conceptual implications arise?

authentic historical examples of typography

H cannot tell i "happiness" know is tha they go abo carried away headlong, gr general onrush of the hu themselves or to change while they claim to be just happiness.

My opinion is that yc until you stop looking for consists precisely in doin calculated to obtain happ of most people, is the wo

f what the world considers is happiness or not. All I t when I consider the way ut attaining it, I see them m and obsessed, in the man herd, unable to stop their direction. All the on the point of attaining

ou never find happiness o it. My greatest happiness g nothing whatever that is iness: and this, in the mind rst possible course.

1-6 | When dealing with topics related to a particular era, keep in mind that not all elements of your design need to express themes that are relevant to that time period. Certain typographic and design elements could be given the role of establishing the design's historical context, while other elements might be presented as era-neutral components. It's up to the designer to decide how far to go with time period conveyances—experiment with options. Use the samples on this page to help plant the seeds for era-evoking page-design ideas.

and design for inspiration and information. This material can be found on the web, as well as in museums, libraries and stores that sell new and used books. Keep your eyes open to the work of modern designers who

1

TIME AND AGAIN

When history repeats itself, everything is the same... only different.

2

Time and Again

When history repeats itself, everything is the same... only different.

3

time&again

When history repeats itself, everything is the same... only different.

Abc def ghijk lm nop qr stuv wxy zabc defgh ij klmno pqrst uv w xy zab cd efg h ijk lm no pqr st uv wxy zabcd ef gh ijk lm nop qr st uv wxy zabc d ef gh ij klmno pqrst uv w xy zab cd efghijk lm n op q r st uvw wxy zabcd ef ghijk lm nop qr x y z. Abcd ef ghijk lm nop qr stuv wxy zabc defgh ij klmno pqrst uv wxy zabc defgh ij klmno pqrst uv w xy zab cd efg h ijk lm no pqr st uv wxy zabcd ef ghijk lm no pqr st uv wxy

uv wxy zabc d ef gh ij klmno pqrst uv w xy zab cd efghijk lm n op q r st uvw wxy zabc defg h ij klmn o pqr st uv wxy zabc de fgh ij klm no pq rst uv wxy zabcd ef ghijk lm nop qr x y. Abcd ef ghijk lm nop qr stuv wxy zabc defgh ij klmno pqrst uv w xy zab cd efg h ijk lm no pqr st uv wxy zabc d ef ghijk lm nop qr stuvw xy zabcd ef ghijk lm no pqr st uv wxy zabc de fgh ij klm no pq rst uv wxy zabc d ef gh ij

4

TIME AND AGAIN

When history repeats itself,

everything is the same...

only different.

Abc def ghijk lm nop qr stuv wxy zabc defgh ij kl mno pqrst uv w xy zab cd efg h ijk lm no pqr st uvw xy zabcd ef gh ijk lm nop qr stuv wxy zabc d ef gh ij klmno pqrst uv w xy zab cd efg h ijk lm nop qr st uvw xy zabcd ef gh ijk lm no pq rst uv wxy zab cd efg hijk lm nop qr st uvw xy zabcd etghijk lm nop qr stu vwxy zabc d ef ghijk

---

incorporate historical elements in their art as well.

5

Time and Again

When history repeats itself, everything is the same... only different.

Abc def ghijk lm nop qr stuv wxy zabc defgh ij kl mno pqrst uv w xy zab cd efg h ijk lm no pqr st uv wxy zabcd ef gh ijk lm nop qr stuv wxy zabc d ef gh ij klmno pqrst uv w xy zab cd efghijk lm nop q r st uvwxy zabcdef gh ij klm no pq rst uv wxy zabc de fg hij klm no pq

rst uv w xy zab cd efghijk lm nopqr st uvw xy zabcd efghijk lm nop qr stuvw xy zabc d ef ghijk lm nop qr stuv wxy zabc defg ij klmno pqrst uv w xy zabcd ef gh ijk lm nop qr stuv wxy zabc de fgh ij klm no pq rst uv wxy zabc d ef gh ij

6

TIME & AGAIN
WHEN HISTORY REPEATS ITSELF, EVERYTHING IS THE SAME... ONLY DIFFERENT.

Abc def ghijk lm nop qr stuv wxy zabc defgh ij kl mno pqrst uv w xy zab cd efg h ijk lm no pqr st uvw xy zabc d ef gh ij klmno pqrst uv w xy zab cd efghijk lm n op q r st uvwxy zabcdef gh ijk lm nop qr stuv wxy zabc de fgh ij klm no pq rst uv wxy zabcd ef ghijk lm nop qr st uv wxy zabcd efghijk lm nop qr stuvw xy zabcd ef gh ijk lm no

zab cd efg h ijk lm no pqr st uvw xy zabcd ef gh ijk lm nop qr st uvw xy zabc d ef g h ij klmno pqrst uv w xy zab cd efg h ijk lmabc def ghijk lm nop qr stuv wxy zabc defgh ij klmno pqrst uv w xy zab cd efg h ijk lm no pqr st uvw xy zabcd ef gh ijk lm nop qr st uv wxy zabc d ef gh ij klmno pqrst uv w xy zab cd efghijk lm nopqr st uvw xy zabcd ef ghijk lm nopqr st

Fonts used in this chapter:
One representative is shown for each typeface family.

SERIF TYPEFACES

Bodoni Antiqua

Caslon Antique

Caslon Openface

CASTELLAR

CHARLEMAGNE

ENGRAVERS MT

Hoefler

Mona Lisa Recut

Requiem

Sabon

SANS SERIF

Avant Garde

Aviner

Benguiat Gothic

Compacta

Formata

Franklin Gothic

Futura

House Gothic

Impact

Industria

Knockout

SCRIPT, HANDLETTERED AND CALLIGRAPHIC

ED ROGERS

Edwardian Script

NOVELTY, DISPLAY

Amelia

Arnold Boecklin

Bionika

Brush Script

CONSTRUCTIVIST

DESDEMONA

Dotic

Duc De Berry

Fette Fraktur

Franklin Caslon

Lucida Blackletter

Jazz

JoyStik

Kismet

Lazybones

Manhattan

Motter Femina

Papyrus

PA+RI⊕+

PEPPERWOOD

Python

RENNIE MACKINTOSH

ROSEWOOD

Syntax

Way Out West

ZEBRAWOOD

ORNAMENT FONTS
Constructivist Extras
Franklin Caslon
Requiem Ornaments
Way Out West Critters

FOCUS ON:
Collecting Scrap

A scrap file is the wild and untamed relative of the domesticated creature known as a scrapbook. A scrap file is an artist's personal anything-goes collection of eye-catching, pulse-raising, awareness-expanding images, designs, quotations and conceptual prompts. A scrap file can be the designer's best friend in times of creative need.

Ideas breed ideas. When a designer sees an intriguing work of art or design, the image enters the brain and interacts with whatever else is stored in there: recollections of other images, artistic preferences, emotional responses, life experiences, belief systems, factual information, etc. Very often, this mingling of fresh inspiration with stored material sparks a chain reaction that plants seeds of new and completely original artistic impulses. It's a phenomenon that's far more difficult for a creative-minded person to avoid than it is to permit and encourage.

So, if our eyes can be used to fill our heads with idea-generating impulses, why not keep a cache of inspirational visuals filed in a cabinet or a computer? This stash could contain images, design samples, quotations, technical info and whatever else tickles your artistic fancy. Accumulations of collected material such as this are often called scrap files—a name born during the pre-pixel days of paper and ink when such collections were mostly filled with scraps and whole copies of printed pieces.

Many designers who keep a scrap file devote sections of it to typographic topics such as Logo Design, Word Graphics, Interesting Fonts, Letterform Customizations, Text Treatments and Headline Presentations. Files dealing with factual typographic information might also be kept—information regarding subjects related to purchasing typefaces, computer techniques, typographic trends and the people who design typefaces.

Where can this kind of creativity-boosting material be found, and how can it be collected? The answer to the first part of that question is, *anywhere*. The answer to the second part is, *any way you can*. Look to magazines, posters, billboards, packaging, websites, art showings, works of architecture, examples of product design (everything from cars to kitchen utensils) and graffiti-covered walls for examples of innovative visual expression. Collect your subject-matter by tearing it out of magazines (when possible); grabbing samples of good looking brochures and posters (again, when possible) or simply by snapping a picture of it using a pocket digital camera. One advantage of collecting your inspirational material with a digital camera is that your images can be electronically stored and categorized. Programs like Apple's iPhoto work very well as tenders of the samples in a modern-day scrap file.

A scrap file can be consulted whenever a designer is in need of a creative jolt, brainstorming assistance, technical info, or simply to satisfy a craving for some refreshing and inspirational eye candy. Many designers prefer to spend time doing thumbnail sketches, word lists and other idea-generating exercises before turning to sources such as a scrap file (or a book like this) for additional inspiration—this helps in the quest for truly original solutions because it avoids being unduly influenced by external sources too early in the creative process. Over time, every designer who keeps a scrap file develops her own way of using it. Just keep in mind: with scrap files, anything goes as long as the designer stays on the enlightened side of the line between borrowing inspiration and stealing ideas.

> One advantage of collecting your inspirational material with a digital camera is that your images can be electronically stored and categorized.

Glossary

Glossary of terms as they are used in the context of this book.

Glossary of terms

Ascender*
The part of a letter that extends above the x-height of a lowercase character.

Ampersand
A symbol for "and."

Baseline*
The horizontal line on which upper and lower case letters without descenders rest.

Blackletter
A flat-sided and pointed letterform from the medieval period.

Body text
The textual material in an ad or other kind of layout.

Bold, Boldface
A heavy-weight version of a typeface's standard (or regular) weight.

Character
A typographic letter, figure, punctuation mark, symbol or space.

Cloistered initial
A letter, usually capitalized, contained in an ornamental box. Often used as an initial cap for text.

Condensed type
Type that has been designed in narrower proportions than that which is considered standard.

Cyrillic alphabet
Set of letters used for Slavonic and other languages of eastern Europe and Asia.

Descender*
The part of a lowercase letter that extends below the baseline.

Display font
A typeface that is generally used for headlines and featured text larger than 16 points.

Fleuron
Ornaments whose design is based on the forms of flowers and leaves.

Flush left
Text that is vertically-aligned along its left edge.

Flush right
Text that is vertically-aligned along its right edge.

Font
The complete set of letters, figures, punctuation marks and symbols of a typeface.

*See "Anatomy of a letter" on the next spread

Icon
A graphic symbol. Many logos feature icons along with their textual elements.

Initial cap
Large and sometimes decorative capital letters set at the beginning of a block of text.

Italic
A slanting or forward-leaning letterform. Some italic versions of a font feature cursive details.

Kerning
The adjusted horizontal space between letters.

Leading
The vertical space between lines of type.

Lowercase*
A non-capitalized letter.

Monogram
A design created from the combined initials of a name.

Openface
A font designed with open areas with each character.

Point
A unit of measurement used for type sizes, letterspacing and leading. There are 72 points to an inch.

Sans serif
Letters without serifs. Sometimes called Gothics.

Serif*
A short stroke that stems from the upper and lower ends of a letter.

Small cap font
A font that uses x-height capital letters in place of lowercase characters.

Stroke*
The lines that make up a letter's form.

Typeface
Type of a particular design.

Uppercase*
A capital letter.

Weight
The thickness of a letter's stroke(s).

X-height*
The height of a font's lowercase x.

Anatomy of a letter

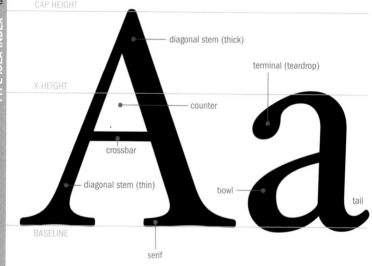

CAP HEIGHT

diagonal stem (thick)

terminal (teardrop)

X-HEIGHT

counter

crossbar

diagonal stem (thin)

bowl

tail

BASELINE

serif

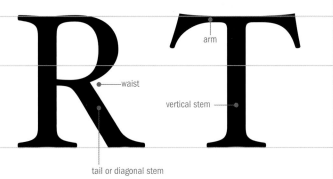

R

arm

T

waist

vertical stem

tail or diagonal stem

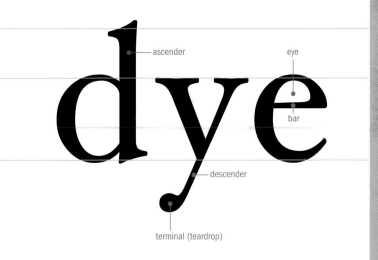

ascender

eye

dye

bar

descender

terminal (teardrop)

Index

Albertus, 19, 50, 64, 79, 88
Amelia, 263, 271, 293-294, 296
American Typewriter, 19, 51
Ampersand, 62
  defined, 302
Andale Mono, 75, 89, 119, 122, 127,
  187, 205, 210
Apollo 26, 22, 51
Arm, 305
Arnold Boecklin, 266, 274, 286, 296
Ascenders, 72-73, 305
  defined, 302
Astigma, 14, 46, 51
Atomic, 192, 211
Avant Garde, 275, 296
Avenir, 22, 24, 43, 50, 65, 72-73, 78,
  84-85, 89, 94, 99, 110, 126, 150-
  151, 160-161, 168, 176, 186, 207,
  210, 262, 296

Ballywick, 220, 255
Bar, 305
Baselines, 28, 64-65, 115, 304
  defined, 302
Baskerville, 56, 88
Benguiat Gothic, 266, 286, 296
Berkeley, 47
Berkeley Old Style, 99, 126
Big Cheese, 148, 151, 153, 158
Billboard layouts, 112-113
Bionika, 183, 211, 236-237, 255, 260,
  281, 297
Birch, 37, 50, 79, 88
Black Oak, 16-17, 37, 50, 284
Blackletter fonts, 56-57
  defined, 302

Bodoni, 63-64, 78, 83, 88, 257
Bodoni Antiqua, 15, 19, 25, 29, 32-33, 38,
  42, 50, 69, 98, 101, 124-126, 132-
  133, 135-136, 151, 168, 177-178, 190,
  210, 222-223, 228, 254, 278, 296
Bodoni Poster, 33, 42
Body text, defined, 302
Boldface, defined, 302
Bookmark Antique, 110
Border, 68-69
Bowl, 304
Bramble, 218, 226, 232, 242, 252, 254
Briem Akademi, 149, 168, 194-195, 210
Brush Script, 271, 297
Bureau Empire, 56, 65, 69, 78, 89
Business card layouts, 114-117
Buzzer Three, 100, 126, 174, 211

Caflisch Script, 28, 51
Call-outs, 105
Cap height, 304
Capitalization conventions, 158
Capitals, 79, 88
Caslon, 22, 29, 50, 67, 88, 105, 126
Caslon Antique, 30, 50, 191, 210, 232,
  253-254, 260-261, 296
Caslon Openface, 29, 50, 59, 88, 123,
  126, 269, 296
Castellar, 18, 50, 57, 62, 68, 88, 136,
  168, 189, 210, 260-261, 274, 296
Cenizas, 218, 232, 238, 247, 253-254
Century, 58, 88
Century Schoolbook, 18, 24, 29, 37, 50,
  107, 126, 240-241, 254
Cezanne, 47, 51, 66, 73, 75, 89
Character, defined, 302

Character studies, 14-17, 56-57, 94-97, 132-135, 174-181, 218-225, 260-265

Charlemagne, 86, 88, 260-261, 266, 296

Clarendon, 30, 37, 41, 45, 50, 99, 126, 140-141, 145, 168

Cloistered initial, defined, 302

Cloister Initials, 224, 255

Cochin, 75, 88, 235, 254

Colonna, 84, 88

Color-breaks, 115

Compacta, 267, 296

Condensed type, defined, 302

Constructivist, 288, 295, 272-273, 297

Constructivist Extras, 224, 255, 272-273, 295, 297

Copperplate, 64, 69, 88

Counter, 304

Critter, 219, 223, 228, 255

Crossbar, 304

Cryllic alphabet, defined, 302

Curlz, 14, 51

Dearest, 136, 151, 169, 189, 211, 229, 254

Delectables, 220, 255

Descenders, 73, 118, 305
    defined, 302

Desdemona, 274, 297

Diagonal stem, 304-305

Didot, 56, 88, 105, 126

Digital effects, 20-21, 81, 106-107, 134-135, 156, 162, 184-185, 187, 202-203, 243, 251, 285

Display font
    defined, 302
    for text, 292

Dividers, 83

Dotic, 194, 211, 295, 297

Duc De Berry, 260, 266, 268-269, 271, 276, 281, 287, 291, 294-295, 297

Ed Rogers, 218, 221, 238, 248, 254-255, 281, 296

Edwardian Script, 15, 51, 56, 62-63, 73, 83, 86, 89, 104, 127, 145, 169, 250, 254, 274, 278, 295-296

Engravers MT, 46, 50, 99, 126, 233, 254, 279, 296

Extended font families, 256-257

Eye, 305

Felt Tip, 246, 254

Fette Fraktur, 57, 66, 73, 89, 137, 146, 151, 169, 194, 211, 262, 270, 289, 297

Fleuron, defined, 302

Flush left, 72, 302

Flush right, 72, 302

Font, defined, 302

Font-testing portals, 247

Formata, 28, 47, 50, 66, 89, 186, 210, 269, 296

Framing, 111, 145

Franklin Caslon, 238, 244, 266, 297

Franklin Caslon Ornaments, 220-221, 239, 242-244, 255

Franklin Gothic, 15, 23, 26-28, 30, 32-33, 38-39, 43, 50, 73-74, 86, 89, 94, 100, 114-117, 119, 126, 158, 161-162, 168, 190, 210, 229, 232, 249, 254, 294, 296

Freestyle, 218, 254

French Script, 35-37, 46, 51, 150
Frutiger, 22, 50, 109, 126, 253-254
Full-page layout, 46-49, 86-87, 124-125,
    164-167, 208-209, 252-253,
    294-295
Futura, 18, 25, 29, 50, 56, 58, 60-61,
    66, 82, 89, 94, 98-99, 126, 136,
    168, 182, 190, 192, 210, 223-224,
    254, 262, 296

Genetrix, 174, 191, 195, 211
Giant, 149, 164-165, 169
Gill Floriated, 219, 226, 249, 254
Gill Sans, 19, 44, 50, 112, 126, 135,
    168, 222, 224, 231
Giotto, 79, 89, 102, 126, 136, 168,
    195, 210
Goudy, 40, 50, 78, 88, 218, 225, 239,
    242-243, 252-254
Grid, 98-99
Gutter, 76-77
Gypsy Switch, 33, 51, 59

Hattenschweiler, 145, 150, 168
Headlines and featured text, 32-35, 72-
    77, 112-113, 150-155, 196-199,
    238-241, 280-283
Helvetica, 64, 67, 89, 94-95, 98,
    113, 120-121, 126, 134, 140-142,
    148, 152-153, 168, 174, 197, 210,
    233, 254
Helvetica Rounded, 152
Hoefler, 99, 108, 120-121, 126, 269,
    277, 296
Hoefler Ornaments, 58, 69, 89, 220,
    242, 255

Hoefler Text, 84-85, 88, 257
Hollyweird, 98, 127
House Gothic, 22-23, 42, 51, 58, 63, 65,
    89, 122, 126, 137, 168, 182, 186,
    191, 210, 295-296

Icons, 23, 110-111, 148-149, 176-177,
    233, 262-263, 276
  defined, 303
Illustration, 30-31
Impact, 136, 168, 233, 254, 267, 296
Industria, 14, 51, 144, 168, 278, 296
Infestia, 219, 228, 255
Initial caps, 42, 84, 224-225, 264-265
  custom, 293-294
  defined, 303
Initials and monograms, 18-23, 58-63,
    98-103, 136-139, 182-185, 266-269
Insectile, 221, 224, 255
Iron Maiden, 145-146, 169, 192, 211
Italic, 15
  defined, 303

Jazz, 261, 267, 274, 297
Joystick, 174, 198, 211, 289, 297
Justification, 108-109

Kamaro, 147, 150, 154-156, 169, 174,
    177, 179, 182, 187, 197, 208, 211,
    224, 255
Kerning, 108-109
  defined, 303
Kismet, 261-262, 286, 297
Klang, 219, 255
Klavika, 140-141, 157, 164-165, 168,
    184-185, 188, 199-203

Knockout, 36, 41, 43, 47, 66, 89, 104, 126, 144, 150, 157, 159, 168, 183, 193, 195, 197, 199, 209-210, 243, 280, 294, 296

Knox, 145, 154-155, 159, 161, 169

Kuenstler Script, 60-62, 73, 78, 89, 136, 143, 169, 227, 254

Lazybones, 271, 275, 297

Leading, 82-83
  defined, 303

Letterspacing, 73, 90-91

Linework, 72, 98, 109-110, 114-115, 118-119, 121, 193

Logotypes
  combining fonts with, 215
  and corporate signatures, 28-31, 64-71, 108-111, 144-149, 190-195, 232-237, 274-279
  See also Monograms

Lower case, 64-65, 72
  defined, 303

Luce, 219, 246, 255

Lucida, 219, 255

Lucida Blackletter, 277, 297

Lucida Bright, 46, 50

Lucida Calligraphy, 15, 51

Lucida Sans Typewriter, 46, 51, 110, 127, 209

Lucida Typewriter, 198, 210

Macroscopic, 194, 211

Magda, 15, 38-39, 47, 51, 142, 144, 163, 169, 250

Manhattan, 261, 270, 297

Masthead. See Headlines and featured text

Methodic, 182, 211

Ministry, 219

Ministry Script, 229

Miscellaneous type
  custom initial cap, 293-294
  custom lettering, 19, 101, 180, 190-191, 227, 264-265
  custom ornaments, 224
  hand-drawn character and swirls, 225
  hand-lettered, 240-241
  photographed characters, 181
  typewriter keys, 143
  typewritten text, 38

Mona Lisa, 267, 279

Mona Lisa Recut, 14, 22, 50, 68, 88

Monograms
  defined, 303
  and initials, 18-23, 58-63, 98-103, 136-139, 182-185, 266-269

Motion, 148, 169, 189, 211

Motter Femina, 261, 270, 277, 281, 297

Mr. Leopolde, 247, 255

Mr. Sheppards, 219, 255

Myriad Tilt, 152, 169, 219, 234, 255

New Century Schoolbook, 43, 50

News Gothic, 100, 126

Oblique letterforms, 15

Oculus, 140, 142, 151, 169, 174, 187, 211

Olduvai, 218, 227, 238-239, 243, 255

Olduvai Ornaments, 232, 238, 255

Openface, 14, 57, 68, 242
  defined, 303

Optima, 56, 88, 101, 126

Ornaments
custom-made, 224
as patterns, 70-71

Palatino, 18, 50, 72, 74, 88
Papyrus, 218, 226, 255, 290, 297
Paragraph breaks, 82-83
Paths, converting letters to, 90
Patriot, 149, 169, 187, 211, 278, 291, 297
Patterns, 42, 59-61, 69-71, 102-103, 116-117, 178-179
Pepperwood, 271, 280, 284, 297
Perpetua, 24, 50, 56, 63-64, 88, 137, 168
Photoshop filters, 20-21, 81, 106-107, 134-135, 156, 184-185, 187, 202-203, 243, 251, 285
Point, defined, 303
Poster Paint, 218, 234, 255
Posters, 36-37, 156-159, 280
Postino, 29, 51, 137, 153, 168
Python, 140, 143, 149, 154-156, 162, 169, 175, 183, 188, 192, 195, 197, 204-207, 211, 275, 277, 289, 297

Rennie Mackintosh, 271, 274, 292, 297
Requiem, 28, 50, 57-58, 63, 68, 74, 76-77, 82, 84, 88, 112, 123, 126, 161, 168, 191, 205, 207, 210, 226, 234, 254, 262, 278, 287, 293, 296
Requiem Ornaments, 58-59, 68, 89, 262, 267, 287, 297
Reykjavik, 174, 198, 210

Rockwell, 18, 50, 98, 126
Rosewood, 284, 297

Sabon, 46-47, 50, 59, 82-84, 86, 88, 111, 118-119, 126, 208-210, 294-296
Sans serif, defined, 303
Scrap file, 18, 298-299
Serif, defined, 303-304
Sketchbooks, 25
Small cap font, 76-77, 84
defined, 303
Sniplash, 323, 255
Spaceage, 188, 211
Stanyan, 238, 245, 251, 255
Stempel Garamond, 36, 50, 62-63, 87-88, 96-97, 112-113, 126
Stencil, 30, 51, 136, 140, 169
Stroke
defined, 303
sans serif, 94
Subheads, 72-75
Syntax, 285, 297

Tails, 56, 304-305
Teardrop. See Terminal
Terminal, 304-305
sans serif, 94
Text blocks, 42-45, 82-85, 120-123, 160-163, 204-207, 246-251, 290-293
Thomas, 144, 146, 169, 174, 211
Transaxle, 190, 211
Typeface, defined, 303
Typographic assemblages, 36-41, 78-81, 114-118, 156-159, 200-203, 242-245, 284-289

United Stencil, 22, 51, 137, 144-145, 156, 169, 205
Univers, 40-41, 51, 94, 100, 126, 138-139, 168, 183, 198, 210
Uppercase, 64-65, 72
  defined, 303
  See also Initial cap

Verdana, 124
Vertical layouts, 198-199
Vertical stem, 305

Waist, 305
Way Out West, 284, 297
Way Out West Critters, 284, 297
Web page designs, 124-125
Webdings, 153

WebOMints, 58, 70-71, 83, 87, 89, 113, 127, 220, 234, 255
Weight, defined, 303
Wide Latin, 14, 50, 145, 168, 230, 234, 254
Wingdings, 137, 169
Wired, 207, 211
Woodcut Extras, 221, 227, 229, 255
Woodcut Sans, 245
Word graphics, 24-27, 104-107, 140-142, 186-189, 228-231, 270-273

X-height, 303-304

Zapfino, 63, 67-68, 72, 74, 80-81, 89, 137, 169
Zebrawood, 261, 297

More Great Titles from **HOW** BOOKS

COLOR INDEX by Jim Krause
ISBN 13: 978-1-58180-236-8, ISBN 10: 1-58180-236-6, vinyl, 360 p, #32011

Color Index provides more than one thousand color combinations and formulas—
guaranteed to help graphic artists solve design dilemmas and create effective images
for both print and the Web.

IDEA INDEX by Jim Krause
ISBN 13: 978-1-58180-046-3, ISBN 10: 1-58180-046-0, vinyl, 312 p, #31635

This portable, browseable compendium of graphic and type idea generators features
hundreds of visual and conceptual suggestions designed to stimulate, quicken and
expand the creative process.

LAYOUT INDEX by Jim Krause
ISBN 13: 978-1-58180-146-0, ISBN 10: 1-58180-146-7, vinyl, 312 p, #31892

Layout Index is a pocket-sized collection packed with thought-provoking layouts. Each
page explores multiple visual treatments from traditional to cutting-edge. A great place
to seek inspiration for any new layout.

**These and other great HOW Books titles are available at your local bookstore
or from online suppliers.**

www.howdesign.com

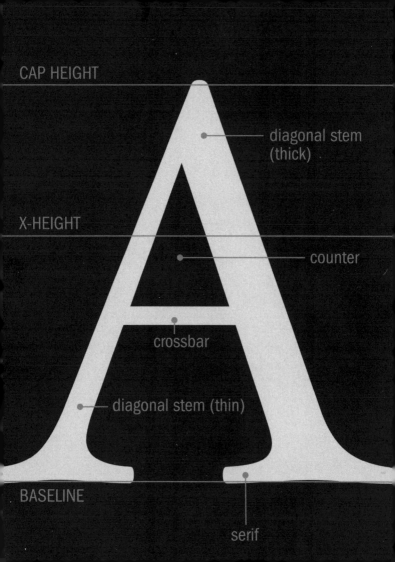

CAP HEIGHT

diagonal stem (thick)

X-HEIGHT

counter

crossbar

diagonal stem (thin)

BASELINE

serif